ISLAM

AND THE FUTURE OF TOLERANCE

ISLAM

AND THE FUTURE OF TOLERANCE

A Dialogue

SAM HARRIS

MAAJID NAWAZ

Harvard University Press

Cambridge, Massachusetts · London, England
2015

Third printing

Library of Congress Cataloging-in-Publication Data
Harris, Sam
Islam and the future of tolerance : a dialogue / Sam Harris,
Maajid Nawaz.
     pages cm
Includes bibliographical references and index.
ISBN 978-0-674-08870-2 (alk. paper)
1. Toleration—Religious aspects—Islam.   2. Dialogue—Religious
aspects.   I. Nawaz, Maajid.   II. Title.
BP171.5.I365 2015
297.2'8—dc23   2015009535

ISLAM

AND THE FUTURE OF TOLERANCE

Harris Maajid, thank you for taking the time to have this conversation. I think the work that you're doing is extremely important. I'm not sure how much we agree about Islam or about the prospects for reforming the faith—and it will be useful to uncover any areas where we diverge—but I want you to know that my primary goal is to support you.

Nawaz That's very kind of you. I appreciate that. As you know, we are working in a very delicate area, walking a tightrope and attempting to bring with us a lot of people who, in many instances, do not want to move forward. It is very important that we have this conversation in as responsible a way as possible.

Harris Agreed. I'd like to begin by recalling the first time we met, because it was a moment when you seemed to be walking this tightrope. It was, in fact, a rather inauspicious first meeting.

In October 2010, I attended the Intelligence Squared debate in which you were pitted against my friends Ayaan Hirsi Ali and Douglas Murray. We met afterward at a dinner for the organizers, participants, and other guests. People were offering short remarks about the debate and otherwise continuing the discussion, and at one point Ayaan said, "I'd like to know whether Sam Harris has anything to say." Although I was well into a vodka tonic at that moment, I remember what I said more or less verbatim. I addressed my remarks directly to you. We hadn't been introduced, and I don't think you had any idea who I was. I said, essentially, this:

> Maajid, I have a question for you. It seems to me that you have a nearly impossible task and yet much depends on your being able to accomplish it. You want to convince the world—especially the Muslim world—that Islam is a religion of peace that has been hijacked by extremists. But the problem is that Islam *isn't* a religion of peace, and the so-called "extremists" are seeking to implement what is arguably the most honest reading of the faith's actual doctrine. So your

maneuvers on the stage tonight—the claims you made about interpretations of scripture and the historical context in which certain passages in the Qur'an must be understood—appear disingenuous.

Everyone in this room recognizes that you have the hardest job in the world, and everyone is grateful that you're doing it. Someone has to try to reform Islam from within, and it's obviously not going to be an apostate like Ayaan, or infidels like Douglas and me. But the path of reform appears to be one of pretense. You seem obliged to *pretend* that the doctrine is something other than it is—for instance, you must pretend that jihad is just an inner spiritual struggle, whereas it's primarily a doctrine of holy war. I'd like to know whether this is, in fact, the situation as you see it. Is the path forward a matter of pretending certain things are true long enough and hard enough so as to *make* them true?

I should reiterate that I was attempting to have this conversation with you in a semipublic context. We weren't being recorded, as far as I know, but there were still around seventy-five people in the room listening to us. I'm wondering if you remember my saying these things and whether you recall your response at the time.

Nawaz Yes, I do remember that. I'm glad you reminded me of it. I hadn't made the connection with you. I'm also grateful you mentioned that although we were not on air, many others were present. To my mind, it was just as important inside that room as outside it for people to take what I was saying at face value. In fact, my desire to impact Muslim-minority societies with my message is just as strong as my desire to impact Muslim-majority societies. Part of what I seek to do is build a mainstream coalition of people who are singing from the same page. That doesn't require that they all become Muslim or non-Muslim. On the contrary, what can unite us is a set of religion-neutral values. By focusing on the universality of human, democratic, and secular (in the British and American sense of this word) values, we can arrive at some common ground. It follows that all audiences need to hear this message. Even inside that room, therefore, the stakes were high. To lose that audience would be to realize my fear: the polarization of this debate between those who insist that Islam is a religion of war and proceed to engage in war for it, and those who insist that Islam is a religion of war and proceed to engage in war against it. That would be an intractable situation.

Now, moving to the specifics of your question, I responded in the way I did because I felt you were implying that I was engaging in pretense by arguing that Islam is a religion of peace. If I remember correctly, you said, "It's understandable in the public context, but here in this room can't you just be honest with us?"

Harris Yes, that's exactly what I said.

Nawaz Yes. "Can't you just be honest with us in here?" implied that I hadn't been honest out there. My honest view is that Islam is not a religion of war *or* of peace—it's a religion. Its sacred scripture, like those of other religions, contains passages that many people would consider extremely problematic. Likewise, all scriptures contain passages that are innocuous. Religion doesn't inherently speak for itself; no scripture, no book, no piece of writing has its own voice. I subscribe to this view whether I'm interpreting Shakespeare or interpreting religious scripture.

So I wasn't being dishonest in saying that Islam is a religion of peace. I've subsequently had an opportunity to clarify at the Richmond Forum, where Ayaan and I discussed this again. Scripture exists;

human beings interpret it. At Intelligence Squared, being under the unnatural constraints of a debate motion, I asserted that Islam is a religion of peace simply because the vast majority of Muslims today do not subscribe to its being a religion of war. If it holds that Islam is only what its adherents interpret it to be, then it is currently a religion of peace.[1]

Part of our challenge is to galvanize and organize this silent majority against jihadism so that it can start challenging the narrative of violence that

---

1. If Islam is largely (or entirely) what Muslims make of it, the state of Muslim public opinion is important to take into account. A 2013 PEW poll conducted in eleven Muslim-majority countries showed that support for suicide bombing against civilians in defense of Islam has declined in recent years. Nevertheless, the numbers of people who still think that this form of violence against noncombatants is "often" or "sometimes" justified are sobering: Egypt (25 percent), Indonesia (6 percent), Jordan (12 percent), Lebanon (33 percent), Malaysia (27 percent), Nigeria (8 percent), Pakistan (3 percent), the Palestinian territories (62 percent), Senegal (18 percent), Tunisia (12 percent), and Turkey (16 percent). There are 1.6 billion Muslims worldwide. If even 10 percent support suicide bombing against civilians in defense of the faith, that's 160 million supporters of terrorism. (www.pewglobal.org)

has been popularized by the organized minority currently dominating the discourse. This is what I was really trying to argue in the Intelligence Squared debate, but the motion forced me to take a side: war or peace. I chose peace.

Harris I understand. My interest in recalling that moment is not to hold you accountable to your original answer to me—and it may be that your thinking has evolved to some degree. But our conversation broke down quite starkly at that point. I don't remember how we resolved it.

Nawaz (laughing) I don't remember that we did resolve it.

Harris Well, let's proceed in a spirit of greater optimism than may seem warranted by our first meeting, because we have a lot to talk about. However, before we dive into the issues, I think we should start with your background, which is fascinating. Perhaps you can tell our readers why you're in a position to know so much about the problems we're about to discuss.

The Roots of Extremism

Nawaz A comprehensive version of my story is available in my autobiography, *Radical,* but I'll summarize it here. I was born and raised in Essex, in the United Kingdom, and grew up in what I refer to as the bad old days of racism in my country. A case that changed the course of race relations in the UK, the murder of Stephen Lawrence, led to a government inquiry that produced the Macpherson report.[2] That report coined the phrase "institutional racism" and judged that it existed in the police forces of the UK. It was a serious indictment.

---

2. The publication of the Macpherson report in February 1999 followed the infamous and racially motivated murder of a young black British teenager, Stephen Lawrence: "It is regarded by many as a defining moment in British race relations . . . The Macpherson report delivered a damning assessment of the 'institutional racism' within the Metropolitan police and policing generally. It made 70 recommendations many aimed specifically at improving police attitudes to racism and stressed the importance of a rapid increase in the numbers of black and Asian police officers." (See http://news.bbc.co.uk/news/vote2001/hi/english/main _issues/sections/facts/newsid_1190000/1190971.stm.)

I came of age at a time immediately preceding that shift in the collective consciousness. I experienced institutional racism on multiple occasions and became incredibly disillusioned with mainstream society as a result. I was falsely arrested on a number of occasions. Such discrimination played out in our young lives while we witnessed the Bosnian genocide unfolding in continental Europe.

Naturally, my generation became disgruntled, disillusioned, and disconnected from society. Into that grave identity crisis came the Islamist ideological group that I eventually joined. The group, Hizb ut-Tahrir, is of the revolutionary variety, remains active across the world, and is still legal in the West. Founded in 1953 in Jerusalem during an earlier Muslim identity crisis after the creation of Israel, Hizb ut-Tahrir was the first Islamist group to popularize the idea of creating a theocratic "caliphate," or an "Islamic state." Rather than terrorism, its members use recruiting and winning over Muslim public opinion, with the eventual aim of inciting military coups in Muslim-majority countries such as Egypt, Turkey, and Pakistan in order to come to power.

I joined this organization as a deeply aggrieved, perhaps traumatized, sixteen-year-old victim of

severely violent racist attacks. However, my grievances were frozen for a long time by the ideological dogma that I came to adopt. I choose my
words here deliberately. Grievances are not in
themselves sufficient to radicalize somebody. They
are half the truth. My meaning is best summa-
rized this way: when we in the West failed to intervene in the Bosnian genocide, some Muslims
became radicalized; when we did intervene in Afghanistan and Iraq, more Muslims became radicalized; when we failed to intervene in Syria, many
more Muslims became radicalized. The grievance
narrative that pins the blame on foreign policy is
only half the story. It is insufficient as an explanation for radicalization.

Harris This topic of foreign intervention and Muslim
grievance is very tricky—and I trust we'll come
back to it. But it seems to me that two things made
the West's intervention in Bosnia unique—and
uniquely inoffensive from a Muslim point of view.
We didn't have to invade a Muslim country to
do it, and the operation entailed bombing *non*-
Muslims. As we've seen from recent conflicts, if
either of those variables changes, a large percentage
of Muslims will view the operation as a sacrilege—

no matter how evil or secular the target of Western power happens to be. Saddam Hussein was the perfect example: he was a universally hated secular tyrant. But the moment a coalition of non-Muslim states attacked him, much of the Muslim world was outraged that "Muslim lands" were being invaded by infidels. Of course, there were many perfectly sane reasons to be against the war in Iraq, but that wasn't among them. One of the problems with religion is that it creates in-group loyalty and out-group hostility, even when members of one's own group are behaving like psychopaths. I would add that when we did eventually intervene in Bosnia, for purely humanitarian reasons, we didn't get much credit for it.

Nawaz Absolutely. I mention it only because where grievances are relevant is in priming young, vulnerable individuals who are experiencing a profound identity crisis to receive ideological dogma through charismatic recruiters. Once that dogma has been received, it frames one's worldview, the lens through which others are perceived, the vehicle by which others are recruited; it becomes the language we speak. It is very important to understand that, because grievances will always exist. They've existed from the beginning of time, and they will exist until the end of time. Other communities face them as well, but this particular ideological phenomenon has arisen only in certain contexts. For example, people often blame poverty or a lack of education for radicalization, whereas experts have long known that a disproportionate number of terrorists come from highly educated backgrounds.[3] So at sixteen I adopted an ideological worldview that froze my sense of grievance and turned it instead into dogma. I then began recruiting heavily for Hizb ut-Tahrir; I bear my fair share of responsibility for promoting the notion of a theocratic caliphate.

Harris Were you seeking to popularize these ideas in the UK or globally?

Nawaz Globally. The group spread from Jerusalem to Jordan, from Jordan to Syria and Iraq, and eventually to Egypt. It then spread from the Middle East to the West, and from the West it spread to Turkey

---

3. See Marc Sageman's study of convicted jihadists in his book *Leaderless Jihad* (Philadelphia: University of Pennsylvania Press, 2008).

via German Muslims, to North Africa via French Muslims, and to South Asia via British Muslims of Indian, Pakistani, and Bangladeshi origin. Becoming an international recruiter, I exported revolutionary Islamism from Britain to Pakistan, Denmark, and, finally, Egypt.

In 1999, midway through my law and Arabic degree at the University of London's School of Oriental and African Studies (SOAS), I took a year off and went to Pakistan on the instructions of Hizb ut-Tahrir to help cofound the Pakistani branch. Pakistan had just tested its atomic bomb a year earlier, and the global leader of our group aspired to a nuclear caliphate.

Anywhere we laid the foundations of this organization, we very specifically targeted army officers so that we could incite military coups. In 2000, after my return from Pakistan, I was personally involved in conversations with Pakistani cadets who had come to study at Britain's Sandhurst Royal Military Academy. Since then, Pakistan has witnessed aborted coup plots by my former organization, some of which have been reported in the press.[4]

---

4. In August 2003 Pakistan's armed forces announced the arrest of several Pakistani officers "sympathetic to extremist

By then, I had resumed study for my degree in London, but I was traveling to Copenhagen every weekend to found the Danish-Pakistani branch of my group. In 2001, my studies took me to Egypt for my Arabic-language year. I arrived one day before the 9/11 attacks. Not fully comprehending the significance of those attacks, I continued recruiting across Egypt for my cause. In April 2002, my Alexandria residence was raided by Egyptian state se-

---

groups." Those arrested were members of Hizb ut-Tahrir who had infiltrated the armed forces. Some of these were members I had personally helped recruit from London in 2000. Upon my return to London in 2006, after my release from prison in Egypt, I met with a British-Pakistani member of Hizb ut-Tahrir, Omar Khan, who had been a ringleader for this Pakistan-based military cell. He confirmed to me that those I had been in touch with were arrested and interrogated alongside him, and while he was deported to Britain, they remained in detention. At that time, Hizb ut-Tahrir was still legal in Pakistan. (See http://www.telegraph.co.uk/news/worldnews/asia/pakistan/1440284/Pakistan-army-officers-arrested-in-terror-swoop.html.) Again, in March 2012, Pakistan's armed forces announced the arrest and foiling of a coup plot led by Brigadier Ali Khan, who was affiliated with Hizb ut-Tahrir. (See http://www.nytimes.com/2012/08/04/opinion/hizb-ut-tahrir-threatens-pakistan-from-within.html?_r=0.)

curity officers. I was blindfolded, had my hands tied behind my back, and was taken to state security headquarters in Cairo, where I witnessed other prisoners being tortured by electrocution. I was twenty-four years old.

After I was sentenced to five years as a political prisoner in Egypt's Mazra Tora prison complex, Amnesty International took the brave step of adopting me as a prisoner of conscience. Although Amnesty disagreed with what we believed in, its view was that we had committed no specific crime in Egypt—which was true—and my group was legal in Britain, where I had joined it. It was in Egypt, in prison with the entire spectrum of Islamists—from the assassins of Egypt's former president Anwar Sadat to the now incarcerated global leader of Egypt's Muslim Brotherhood, Muhammad Badei—that I began to truly explore the ideology I had come to adopt and the cause I had embraced with such fervor at sixteen.

It was a combination of my lengthy revisionist conversations with other prisoners and Amnesty's outreach that started me on the long journey toward a liberal, human rights–based secular perspective. In 2006, I was released from prison and returned to London. In 2008, while completing my master's degree in political theory at the London School of Economics, I cofounded and went on to chair Quilliam, the world's first counter-extremism organization.

The Scope of the Problem

Harris In your work, you make a distinction between "revolutionary Islamists" and "jihadists." I think we should define these terms. I would also like to know how you think public opinion is divided in Muslim communities. I picture several concentric circles: At the center are groups like the Islamic State,[5] al-Qaeda, al-Shebab, Boko Haram, and so on. Their members apparently wake each morning yearning to kill infidels and apostates. Many of them also seem eager to be martyred in the process. Most of

---

5. We have chosen to use the name "the Islamic State" without prejudice, simply because that is what the group calls itself, and this is increasingly how it is referred to in the media. Our usage is not a judgment about the validity of this group's claims to represent the "true" Islam or to have established a caliphate. This book is itself a broader examination of the validity of such claims.

us refer to these people as "jihadists." Then there is a larger circle of Islamists who are more politically motivated and appear less eager to kill and be killed. Beyond that is a wider circle of Muslims who probably support jihad and Islamism—financially, morally, or philosophically—but are not inclined to get their hands dirty. Finally, one hopes, there is a much larger circle of so-called moderate Muslims, whether they would label themselves that way or not, who want to live by more modern values. Although they may not be quite secular, they don't think that groups like the Islamic State represent their faith. Perhaps there are also millions of truly secular Muslims who just don't have a voice. I'm wondering whether you think my understanding of these categories is correct, and if so, what percentage of the earth's 1.6 billion Muslims you would put into each of them.

Nawaz Obviously, this won't be an empirical answer, but I'll give you my gut reaction. Continuing with your concentric-circles imagery, in the center, as you have rightly said, are the jihadists. Beyond them is a larger group of Islamists. So that there's absolutely no confusion for our readers, when I say "Islamism," I mean the desire to impose any given interpretation of Islam on society. When I say "jihadism," I mean the use of force to spread Islamism.

Islamism and jihadism are *politicized, contemporary readings* of Islam and jihad; they are not Islam and jihad per se. As I've said, Islam is a traditional religion like any other, replete with sects, denominations, and variant readings. But *Islamism* is the desire to impose any of those readings on society. It is commonly expressed as the desire to enforce a version of *shari'ah* as law.

Political Islamists seek to impose their views through the ballot box, biding their time until they can infiltrate the institutions of society from within. Revolutionary Islamists seek change from outside the system in one clean sweep. Militant Islamists are jihadists.

It is true that no traditional reading of jihad can ignore the idea of armed struggle, and it is incredibly naive to insist that Muslims ever held jihad to mean an inner struggle *only.* However, any and all armed struggles, in any or no religious contexts, can be defensive or offensive, just or unjust, reactive or preemptive, and terroristic or conventionally militaristic. My usage of jihadism refers only to a particular armed struggle, regardless of which sub-category it fits into above: that which seeks to spread Islamism.

These are only my definitions; in my life working in this field I have yet to come across any that seem more accurate. Others will have their own.

Harris So an Islamist attempts to impose his version of Islam on the rest of society, and a jihadist is an Islamist who attempts to do so by force.

Nawaz That's right.

Harris That clarification is very helpful.

Nawaz Let's move now to your concentric circles. At the center of the inner circle at the moment is the Islamic State, which has come to eclipse al-Qaeda. Its members are what I call global jihadists. Then you have more regional jihadists. They, too, use force to spread Islamism, but they tend to restrict themselves to both a geographic and a demographic focus, and they are less unhinged. Hamas and Hizbollah are in this category. Jihadists are, by anyone's account, a minority of Muslims in the world, but they are the most organized and have the most power, and they dominate the discourse because they're violent. The Islamic State controls huge chunks of territory, and it can raise millions of dollars a day through oil revenues, extortion, and smuggling.

Beyond the jihadists are the remaining Islamists, a much larger group. First come revolutionary Islamists, who are closer to jihadists in their theory, and then come political Islamists, who form the majority of all Islamists yet are still a minority among Muslims. As we witnessed in the first round of elections in Egypt, the Muslim Brotherhood gained only 25 percent of the vote. Second place was claimed by Mubarak's former prime minister, Ahmed Shafik, with 24 percent. That 1 percent margin was insufficient for the Brotherhood to claim victory. In the presidential runoff between Shafik and Mohamed Morsi, despite the certain protest vote against Shafik (who was tainted by affiliation with the previous regime), the Brotherhood still managed to gain only 51 percent of the vote. That suggests that many Egyptians voted for the Muslim Brotherhood in the second round only to prevent the return of Mubarak's former prime minister. It is reasonable to estimate, therefore, that at the height of its power, the world's oldest and largest

Islamist group could muster only about 25 percent in dedicated support.

Harris What percentage of Muslims worldwide are Islamists, in your estimation?

Nawaz I'm using Egypt as an example because that's where the Muslim Brotherhood is particularly successful. And if the Brotherhood in Egypt could gain only 25 percent in the first round of elections, it's probably less popular in other Muslim-majority societies. This is what my gut tells me; I have no empirical evidence.

Harris Actually, one group analyzed the past forty years of parliamentary elections in Muslim-majority countries and found that on average, Islamist parties have carried 15 percent of the vote.[6] This suggests that 15 percent of the world's Muslims are Islamists. However, poll results on the topic of *shari'ah* generally show much higher levels of support for its implementation—killing adulterers,

---

6. C. Kurzman and I. Naqvi, "Do Muslims Vote Islamic?" *Journal of Democracy* 21, no. 2 (April 2010).

cutting off the hands of thieves, and so forth. I'm not sure what to think about a society in which 15 percent of people vote for an Islamist party, but 40 percent or even 60 percent want apostates killed.[7] If nothing else, that would seem to nudge the proportion of Islamists a little higher. I've been saying that the number is probably around 20 percent worldwide—an estimate I consider fairly conservative, whereas Muslim apologists consider it an outrageous fiction that testifies to my bigotry and paranoia.

Nawaz I think it would be extremely helpful if people focused on the ideas being discussed here, rather than on calling you names—which is an easy way to ignore your ideas. Besides, using Egypt as an example, I just estimated the proportion of Islamists worldwide as slightly below 25 percent (keeping in mind that the Muslim Brotherhood reached its peak at 25 percent in Egypt), so I don't think you're that far off the mark. For me, any society in

---

7. Muslim public opinion on the implementation of *shari'ah* has been polled extensively. For instance, http://www.pew forum.org/2013/04/30/the-worlds-muslims-religion-politics -society-beliefs-about-sharia/.

which 15 to 20 percent of the people vote for Islamists is a society facing a severe identity crisis, still struggling to come to terms with the challenges of globalization.

As for your point about higher percentages of support when Muslims are asked specifically about issues such as death for apostasy, I believe that may be rooted in an archaic interpretation of *shari'ah*. But for the sake of my definitions, I would not classify such fundamentalists as Islamists. Their support of death for apostates hails more from a medieval, tribal desire to punish the "out-group," which is justified by religious scripture, than from a belief in the Islamist ideological project of codifying *shari'ah* as law and imposing it on society. This is not to say that such attitudes are healthy—on the contrary, they are incredibly problematic. It's just that they pose a different and sometimes overlapping set of problems *in addition* to Islamism.

In fact, in many instances these same fundamentalists have been known to violently oppose Islamists, considering them entirely a product of Western modernity born from Western innovations of codifying law in unitary legal systems. A case in point is the well-documented conservative movement against the political Islamist group Jamat-e-Islami in the Indian subcontinent during the partition of Pakistan. The Barelvis would chant an anti-Semitic Urdu slogan against the Jamat's founder, Mawdudi—*"Sau yahudi aek Mawdui,"* or "Mawdudi is worse than a hundred Jews." Though despicable, this slogan highlights my point about the animosity between many fundamentalists and Islamists. Mumtaz Qadri, who assassinated Salmaan Taseer, the blasphemy-law reformer and governor of Punjab in Pakistan, hailed from this same Barelvi movement.

That leads perfectly to the next circle, which is by far the largest: religiously conservative Muslims. Whether one looks to Pakistan, Indonesia, Malaysia, Egypt, or the Gulf, the majority of Muslims are currently conservative—some would call them fundamentalists. Let's call them conservatives, because they don't wholeheartedly subscribe to contemporary liberal human rights.

Harris What is the line between conservative Islam and Islamism? In other words, what keeps conservatives from wanting to impose Islam on the rest of society?

Nawaz Oh, many things. Let's take Egypt again as an example. Egypt is a conservative religious country, yet the vast majority of Egyptian Muslims eventually rejected the Muslim Brotherhood government, expressing themselves in perhaps the largest protest in that country's history. In doing so they were backed by many Egyptian theologians. Unfortunately, those protests ended in a populist military coup, rather than another election, to oust the Brotherhood. This reinforces my point that although conservative Egyptians didn't choose liberal secular democracy, they did resoundingly reject the Muslim Brotherhood.

Tunisia provides another example. The 2014 election there resulted in Muslim Arab Tunisians rejecting the Nahda party's government—a party with Islamist roots—and voting in a secular party instead. The good news is that the Nahda party abdicated peacefully, even publicly endorsing the will of the people as sovereign.

Most traditional Muslims consider Islamism an errant politicization of their religion. These people are extremely conservative in their own families and lifestyles—they do pose certain core human rights challenges—but they generally don't want the state to impose their religion, because they want to retain the right to have their own understanding of what this religious conservatism means.

Harris Very interesting. So when we talk about a phenomenon like honor killing, we're not just worried about Islamists; we're worried about how the average conservative Muslim man will treat his wife or daughter in light of his religious beliefs and cultural values. And yet many of these conservatives may be opponents of Islamism.

Nawaz Yes. Conservative Muslims can be very useful as allies against Islamism and jihadism, but they may oppose you on gender rights and equality and, in some cases, honor killings. So the subject at hand will affect whether or not they ally with you.

Conservative Muslims can be very vocal against al-Qaeda, for instance, because they believe al-Qaeda is hijacking their religion. The vast majority of Muslims in, say, Saudi Arabia, Indonesia, Pakistan, and Egypt are conservative. This complicates matters, because we're currently faced with two entirely different challenges—facing down Islamism and jihadism on the one hand, and advancing human rights and democratic culture on the other. Conservative Muslims may be our allies for the former but not the latter. This puts reform-minded liberal Muslims in a really, really difficult situation.

Harris That's another extremely helpful distinction.

Nawaz Recall that I classified the majority of Muslims as conservative: though not all conservatives may be "practicing" Muslims, their views tend to reflect traditional Muslim values. Well, a smaller group beyond those are reform Muslims—people like the UK's lead reform theologian, Dr. Usama Hasan. They are attempting both to challenge Islamism head-on and to reform some of the more conservative interpretations of the faith. By "reform" I mean renew or update interpretations, not with any specific reference to the Christian Reformation. These reformists are, I believe, the cream of the crop in terms of having the networks and the intelligence to approach this discussion. I hope they are the future, and if I have anything to do with it, they will be.

As mentioned, I cofounded and run Quilliam, the world's first counter-extremism organization, based in London. It is our unenviable task to challenge those who resort to Islamist or other forms of cultural extremism and to promote secular democratic counter-messages. Quilliam is a secular organization, but by pointing to historical and contemporary pluralism in scriptural reasoning, we can challenge the rigidity of violent, fundamentalist, or ideological dogma. We are a registered charity in the US and rely on grants and donations to survive. With the help of Islamic theologians like Dr. Hasan, we tackle the two challenges I just mentioned of Islamism and overly conservative religious dogma, promoting human rights and democratic culture as an interpretative framework. In doing so, we have sometimes upset conservative Muslims, who started off as our allies against Islamists. If we hadn't addressed human rights issues, they still would be. However, we can't remain silent on gender rights and personal freedoms. It is very difficult, but we are duty-bound to try to bring some of them closer to the reform discourse—while also trying to address those at the other end of the spectrum, who have become virulently anti-Muslim.

My holding this dialogue with you may in itself cause concern among some conservative and some tribal (yet nonreligious) Muslims. Whereas I see our conversation as a prime example of how the fog can be lifted if we simply put aside the hyperbole and ditch the posturing, others will view it as fraternizing with the enemy—that enemy being you. My principles allow me to have this dialogue with you, despite your views about Islam and its negative role in today's world, just as they would allow me to have a dialogue with members of the Muslim Brotherhood, who advocate "Islam is the solution" for today's world. In either case, my aim would be to further my secular, democratic, human rights values. In fact, I regularly exchange views with committed Islamists and jihadists in an attempt to bring them away from their ideological dogma— as is my role. Yet I suspect that for many conservative or tribal (yet nonreligious) Muslims, my talking to you is more problematic than my talking to jihadists. That highlights the extent of the problem we face today.

Harris It does indeed.

Nawaz Now, when I talk about the sizes of these various circles we've just categorized, it's very important to know that I'm referring to them in a global sense. America in particular may be different. For example, I think Muslims have tended to integrate better in America than they have in Britain. I don't want our readers to think that the vast majority of American Muslims must be conservative. There is a strong reform strand within US Muslim discourse, and it may be that most American Muslims support it.

Another, smaller group is what I would call "citizens who happen to be Muslim." The difference between them and reformist Muslims is that many people out there don't identify primarily as Muslim when interacting with society. It happens to be one of their cultural identities, but it's not first and foremost. I'm deliberately not using the term "secular Muslim" here, because of course conservative and reformist Muslims may be secular too.

Harris In fact, you're using a more precise definition of the word "secular" than is common in this context. To spell it out for our readers: secularism is simply a commitment to keeping religion out of politics and public policy. Your religion is your business, and my religion, or lack of one, is mine. A willingness to build a wall of separation between church and state is what defines secularism—but, as you point out, behind that wall one may be a full-blown religious fanatic, so long as one doesn't try to impose the fruits of one's fanaticism on others.

Nawaz Indeed, and secular religious people may still reject a human rights discourse to a degree—a state of affairs that I would not be satisfied with. What I hope is that people will arrive not just at secularism, but also at democratic and human rights values. So the task ahead of us is monumental, but secularism is the prerequisite. This is a unique challenge for Muslims today owing to the rise of Islamism and jihadism, and to the historically European context in which secularism is framed. This challenge is not, however, insurmountable.

Ideally, I'd like all Muslims to be either reform-minded or citizens who happen to be Muslims. You won't hear from that last group, however. They're not going to come to you and say, "Hey, Sam, I don't believe in all that and I'm Muslim," because they're not engaging with society as Muslims. They are lawyers, doctors, caretakers, cleaners, and drivers. If all these people became just "citizens" and interacted with their political structures through their elected representatives, most of the problem would be solved.

Finally, some remarks on the term "moderate" Muslim. After the Islamic State, even al-Qaeda appears "moderate." The term is so relative—juxtaposed against increasingly worse atrocities—that it has become meaningless. It doesn't tell us which values the person in question holds. This is why I prefer using terms that denote values, such as "Islamist," "liberal," or "conservative" Muslim.

Harris Your intuitions about the relative sizes of these groups certainly track my own. As I've said, we have a fair amount of polling data on the question of what Muslims believe. I'd like to know what you make of these data. Specifically, the polls that were done in Britain immediately after the 7/7 bombings in London revealed that more than 20 percent of British Muslims felt sympathy for the bombers' motives; 30 percent wanted to live under *shari'ah*; 45 percent thought that 9/11 was the result of a conspiracy between the United States and Israel; and 68 percent believe that British citizens who "insult Islam" should be arrested and prosecuted.[8]

---

8. http://www.cbsnews.com/news/many-british-muslims-put -islam-first/.

To learn that 78 percent of *British* Muslims think anyone who published the Danish cartoons should have been punished—and surely some significant number would have wanted them killed—is extremely troubling. Perhaps you could say a few words about the specific situation in Britain.

Nawaz Yes, those poll figures are indeed troubling—with the caveat that "live under *shari'ah*" can mean different things to different respondents. We at Quilliam are based in London, and we say this openly, though it doesn't make us very popular among many of my co-religionists: by comparison with America, Britain has a disproportionately large problem with Muslim extremism, as does Europe. A more recent poll indicates that 27 percent of Britain's Muslims said that they had some sympathy for the motives behind the Charlie Hebdo attacks in Paris. Eleven percent felt sympathy for people who wish to fight against "Western interests."[9] Though this poll establishes that the majority hold less sympathy for violence, these two figures are still alarmingly high in a

---

9. http://www.bbc.co.uk/news/uk-31293196.

context where up to 1,000 British Muslims may have gone to fight for the Islamic State.

Harris Would you say that Britain is the most challenging country in Europe in this respect?

Nawaz Although Belgium has the highest percentage of citizens who recently went to Iraq and Syria to join the Islamic State, studies show that the 500 to 1,000 who left from Britain have a higher level of education and can be more extreme than their European counterparts.[10] Such numbers point to an uncomfortably large minority and could not have emerged from a vacuum. In fact, one of the most alarming polls reported recently by the London *Times* found that one in every seven young Britons has "warm feelings" toward the Islamic State.[11] Whether or not this is accurate, it suggests a level of grassroots sympathy that is too high for comfort. An ideological undercurrent within communities

---

10. T. Coghlan, "British jihadists wealthier and better educated than those from rest of Europe," *The Times*, October 2, 2014.

11. O. Moody, "One in seven young Britons has sympathy with Isis cause," *The Times*, October 30, 2014.

fosters these numbers. Britain has become a net exporter of Islamism and jihadism. My former Islamist group didn't exist in Pakistan until we exported it from Britain.

So we've got a serious problem in the UK and across Europe, and I'm not making any excuses for that. We set up Quilliam to meet this challenge head-on. We attempt, first and foremost, to isolate jihadists from everyone else and then to challenge Islamists and distinguish them from conservatives and other Muslim communities. We encourage Muslims to start seeing political Islamism for what it is: a modern ideology that first emerged with the Muslim Brotherhood. We also address Muslim communities in the UK on the broader need to wholeheartedly subscribe to democratic, human rights–based reform. That's a huge challenge just in Europe, let alone the rest of the world. So we need all the help we can get.

The Power of Belief

Harris To return to your personal story for a moment, your Islamism seems to have been primarily political, borne of some legitimate grievances—

primarily racial injustice—that you began to view through the lens of Islam. But you haven't said, as members of al-Qaeda do, that you were incensed by the sacrilege of infidel boots on the ground near Muslim holy sites on the Arabian Peninsula. To what degree did *religious* beliefs—a desire for martyrdom, for instance—motivate you and your fellow Islamists? And if no such ideas were operative, can you discuss the religious difference between a revolutionary Islamist outlook and a jihadist one?

Nawaz Yes, sure, of course. There are indeed similarities and differences between Islamism and jihadism. We shouldn't be surprised by this—the same applies when we look at, say, communism. Socialists are on one end, and communists on the other; some are militant, and some aren't. It's the same with Islamism.

Now, I've argued that the motivation for Islamists *and* jihadists is ideological dogma, fed to them by charismatic recruiters who play on a perceived sense of grievance and an identity crisis. In fact, I believe that four elements exist in all forms of ideological recruitment: a grievance narrative, whether real or perceived; an identity crisis; a charismatic recruiter; and ideological dogma. The dogma's "narrative" is its propaganda.

The difference between Hizb ut-Tahrir and al-Qaeda is akin to the dispute within communism as to whether change comes from direct action and conflict.

If you take the theory of dialectical materialism in communism—and whether we should step back and allow the course of history to carve its own way or intervene to affect it—purists of that theory will argue that you don't have to do anything, that the means of production will naturally shift from the bourgeoisie to the workers, and any intervention is futile because that's just the way history works. Others will say we must take direct action.

Such differences on a theoretical level also exist between Islamists of the political (or "entryist") type, those of the revolutionary type, and jihadists. Of course, jihadists believe in taking direct action; they have an entire theory around that. I'd argue, in fact, that the rise of the so-called Islamic State under Abu Bakr al-Baghdadi does somewhat vindicate Osama bin Laden's strategy and his belief that making the West intervention-weary through war would lead to a power vacuum in the Middle

East and that the West would abandon its support for Arab despots, which would lead to the crumbling of despotic regimes. From the ashes of that would rise an Islamic State. Bin Laden said this eleven years ago, and it's uncanny how the Arab uprisings have turned out.

Harris What I'm trying to get at is the religious distinction I *think* I detect between the type of Islamist you were—having been the victim of violent prejudice in the UK and becoming politically radicalized by Islam—and someone who may or may not have similar grievances but decides to go fight for a group like the Islamic State because he genuinely believes that he's participating in a cosmic war against evil, and will either spread the one true faith to the ends of the earth or get himself martyred in the process. Were you thinking about the prospects of your own martyrdom? Or was your Islamism more a matter of politics and ordinary grievances?

Nawaz I suppose I'm trying to say that although there's a difference in methodology, all Islamists believe they're engaged in a cosmic struggle; but this cosmic struggle isn't the *only* reason they're doing it.

Harris Perhaps I'm giving too much credit to critics of my views on this topic, but let me bend over backward once more. I'm imagining (as so many people insist is the case) that some significant percentage of highly dedicated Islamists are *purely* political, in that they're motivated by terrestrial concerns and are simply using Islam as the banner under which to promote their cause. Aren't there Islamists who *don't* believe in the metaphysics of martyrdom?

Nawaz We would simply call them insincere. Insincere people exist in any movement and under any ideology. But if we're going to look at what Islamists subscribe to, obviously we have to discount the minority who are Machiavellian and join only because they want something else out of it.

But if you consider those who are sincere—and I was sincere in what I used to believe—you'll find that they're prepared for martyrdom. I had to face torturers in Egypt and thought I was going to die for my cause. In that sense all sincere Islamists believe they're engaged in a cosmic struggle for good against evil, and they define "good" as a holy struggle. But again, to emphasize, that is not the *only* thing they believe.

Though they do certainly believe in martyrdom, they also believe in the "evils" of Western imperialism. Likewise, they believe that they're living under Arab dictators. The grievance narrative kicks in, as I said, prior to the point of recruitment. But at the point of recruitment this grievance narrative is fossilized by ideological dogma, which then becomes the vehicle through which they express themselves. So it's not one or the other. But certainly the cosmic struggle is a consistent element for all Islamists.

Another difference between jihadists and Islamists is that Islamists will seek martyrdom according to their own theory. So in Hizb ut-Tahrir we were taught that martyrdom is achieved by being killed while holding a despotic ruler to account or spreading the ideology. We were taught that if the regime kills you while you're attempting to recruit army officers, you'll be a martyr, and you should embrace that. But we were also taught that you're not a martyr if you blow yourself up in a marketplace, because you're killing civilians and other Muslims.

Now, whereas Hizb ut-Tahrir was attempting to incite coups by the existing army, jihadists simply said, "Why don't we create our own army? Why are we bothering with these guys, who are infidels anyway?" For jihadists, to die while fighting for their own army is martyrdom. That is the difference. As long as you're dying in accordance with the view you subscribe to, you're a martyr in the eyes of your group.

Harris So you wouldn't distinguish between jihadists and other Islamists as to *degree* of religious conviction—for instance, their level of certainty about the existence of paradise or the reality of martyrdom? The difference is purely a matter of methodology?

Nawaz Yes. Some jihadists are not "pious" in the sense of having firm religious convictions. They simply prefer the violence, the direct action, so they're attracted to those groups. Yet some Islamists are incredibly pious and sincerely believe in the holiness of their *political* cause. So piety or the lack of it, and religious sincerity or the lack of it, fluctuates between, within, and among groups.

Harris This is all fascinating—and, again, extremely useful to spell out. But we should clarify another point here, because the line between piety and its lack may not be detectable in the way many of our readers expect. For instance, it's often suggested that the 9/11 hijackers couldn't have been true believers, because they went to strip clubs before they carried out their suicide mission. However, to me, there's absolutely no question that these men believed they were bound for paradise. I think many people are confused about the connection between outward observance and belief.

Nawaz That's right.

Harris The 9/11 hijackers were not suicidally depressed people who went to strip clubs and then just decided to kill themselves along with thousands of innocent strangers. Whether or not they went to strip clubs, or *appeared* pious in any other way, these men were true believers.

Nawaz Yes. The strip club thing is a red herring, because even in a traditional view of jihad, when you believe you're engaged in an act of war, you're allowed to deceive the enemy. So whether it's espionage, or going undercover, or war propaganda, within traditional thinking—as revived by modern jihadism—it's permissible during war.

The 9/11 hijackers' being seen in strip clubs is, however, relevant for use in propaganda against them. Most conservative Western Muslims (who do not think they're at war with their own countries) would find such behavior irreligious. But you're absolutely right to say that it's not indicative of the hijackers' religious convictions or lack thereof. This confusion between supposed jihadist religiosity and sex should be clearer now after the world has witnessed Boko Haram and the Islamic State's enslavement and mass rape of women.

It is not necessarily accurate to assume that, say, the leaders of the Muslim Brotherhood are somehow less pious than the leaders of, say, the Islamic State. More violence does not necessarily equate with greater religious conviction. Each group is deeply convinced of its approach to achieving Islamism in society, and both face much danger in pursuit of that goal. But they differ in methodology, and they very much despise each other, just as Trotsky and Stalin eventually did. That didn't mean one was less a communist than the other; they had a factional dispute within their ideology. Some people misunderstand such disputes within Islamism. They argue, "What do you mean Islamism? There's no such thing." The Muslim Brotherhood hates groups like the Islamic State, and the Islamic State would kill members of the Muslim Brotherhood. I always remind them, that's like saying there's no such thing as communism just because Stalin is said to have killed Trotsky. It's an absurd conclusion to reach. Of course there's a thing called communism. And there's a thing called Islamism. It's an ideology. People are seeking to bring it about, but they differ in their approach.

Degrees of religious conviction are not what will help us understand the differences among jihadists, revolutionary Islamists, political Islamists, and non-Islamist Muslims. Let's take Sayyid Qutb, for example. Qutb was a member of the Muslim Brotherhood and is now known as one of the founding fathers of the theory that eventually became modern jihadism. The Egyptian regime killed him for writing a book, which he wrote while incarcerated in the same prison I came to be held in many years later. It takes a high degree of religious conviction to die merely for writing a book, and that, for the Brotherhood, was martyrdom. Likewise, Hizb ut-Tahrir members glorify the death of their members at the hands of the regime, but not the

death of suicide bombers. They prepare their adherents to be killed for trying to overthrow a regime,
and they tell all the same stories about martyrdom
and eternal bliss in paradise that jihadists do.

Harris The only conclusion I can draw from everything you've just said is that the problem of ideology is far worse than most people suppose.

Nawaz Absolutely. But to repeat, ideology is but one
of four factors, albeit the most often ignored.

Harris I would generally agree—although there certainly seem to be many cases in which people have
no intelligible grievance apart from a theological
one and become "radicalized" by the idea of sacri-
ficing everything for their faith. I'm thinking of the
Westerners who have joined groups like al-Qaeda
and the Islamic State, for instance. Sometimes, religious ideology appears to be not merely necessary but *sufficient* to motivate a person to do this.
You might say that an identity crisis was also
involved—but everyone has an identity crisis at
some point. In fact, one could say that the whole of
life is one long identity crisis. The truth is that some
people appear to be almost entirely motivated by

their religious beliefs. Absent those beliefs, their behavior would make absolutely no sense; with them, it becomes perfectly understandable, even rational.

As you know, the public conversation about the connection between Islamic ideology and Muslim intolerance and violence has been stifled by political correctness. In the West, there is now a large industry of apology and obfuscation designed, it would seem, to protect Muslims from having to grapple with the kinds of facts we've been talking about. The humanities and social science departments of every university are filled with scholars and pseudo-scholars—deemed to be experts in terrorism, religion, Islamic jurisprudence, anthropology, political science, and other fields—who claim that Muslim extremism is never what it seems. These experts insist that we can never take Islamists and jihadists at their word and that none of their declarations about God, paradise, martyrdom, and the evils of apostasy have anything to do with their real motivations.

When one asks what the motivations of Islamists and jihadists actually are, one encounters a tsunami of liberal delusion. Needless to say, the West is to

blame for all the mayhem we see in Muslim societies. After all, how would *we* feel if outside powers
and their mapmakers had divided our lands and
stolen our oil? These beleaguered people just want
what everyone else wants out of life. They want
economic and political security. They want good
schools for their kids. They want to be free to
flourish in ways that would be fully compatible
with a global civil society. Liberals imagine that jihadists and Islamists are acting as anyone else
would given a similar history of unhappy encounters with the West. And they totally discount the
role that religious beliefs play in inspiring a group
like the Islamic State—to the point where it would
be impossible for a jihadist to prove that he was
doing *anything* for religious reasons.

Apparently, it's not enough for an educated
person with economic opportunities to devote
himself to the most extreme and austere version of
Islam, to articulate his religious reasons for doing
so ad nauseam, and even to go so far as to confess
his certainty about martyrdom on video before
blowing himself up in a crowd. Such demonstra-
tions of religious fanaticism are somehow considered rhetorically insufficient to prove that he really

believed what he said he believed. Of course, if he said he did these things because he was filled with despair and felt nothing but revulsion for humanity, or because he was determined to sacrifice himself to rid his nation of tyranny, such a psychological or political motive would be accepted at face value. This double standard is guaranteed to exonerate religion every time. The game is rigged.

I don't know if you're familiar with the same liberal apologists I am. Some are journalists, some are academics, a few are Muslims—but the general picture is of a white, liberal non-Muslim who equates any criticism of Islamic doctrines with bigotry, "Islamophobia," or even "racism." These people are very prominent in the US, and their influence is as intellectually embarrassing as it is morally problematic. Although they don't make precisely the same noises on every question, they deny any connection between heartfelt religious beliefs and Muslim violence. Whole newspapers and websites can now be counted on to function as de facto organs of Islamist apology—*The Guardian, Salon, The Nation, Alternet,* and so forth. This has made it very difficult to have public conversations of the sort we are having.

The Betrayal of Liberalism

Nawaz Yes, we have such debates in the UK as well. Everything I'm going to say from here on I say as a liberal—in fact, I say while being a Liberal Democrat parliamentary candidate in London. A great liberal betrayal is afoot. Unfortunately, many "fellow-travelers" of Islamism are on the liberal side of this debate. I call them "regressive leftists"; they are in fact reverse racists. They have a poverty of expectation for minority groups, believing them to be homogenous and inherently opposed to human rights values. They are culturally reductive in how they see "Eastern"—and in my case, Islamic— culture, and they are culturally deterministic in attempting to freeze their ideal of it in order to satisfy their orientalist fetish. While they rightly question every aspect of their "own" Western culture in the name of progress, they censure liberal Muslims who attempt to do so within Islam, and they choose to side instead with every regressive reactionary in the name of "cultural authenticity" and anticolonialism.

They claim that their reason for refusing to criticize any policy, foreign or domestic—other than those of what they consider "their own" government—is that they are not responsible for other governments' actions. However, they leap whenever *any* (not merely their *own*) liberal democratic government commits a policy error, while generally ignoring almost every fascist, theocratic, or Muslim-led dictatorial regime and group in the world. It is as if their brains cannot hold two thoughts at the same time. Besides, since when has such isolationism been a trait of liberal internationalists? It is a right-wing trait.

They hold what they think of as "native" communities—and I use that word deliberately—to lesser standards than the ones they claim apply to all "their" people, who happen to be mainly white, and that's why I call it reverse racism. In holding "native" communities to lesser—or more culturally "authentic"—standards, they automatically disempower those communities. They stifle their ambitions. They cut them out of the system entirely, because there's no aspiration left. These communities end up in self-segregated "Muslim areas" where the only thing their members aspire to is being tinpot community leaders, like ghetto chieftains. The "fellow-travelers" fetishize these "Muslim" ghettos in the name of "cultural authenticity" and identity politics, and the ghetto chieftains are often the leading errand boys for them. Identity politics and the pseudo-liberal search for cultural authenticity result in nothing but a downward spiral of competing medieval religious or cultural assertions, fights over who are the "real" Muslims, ever increasing misogyny, homophobia, sectarianism, and extremism.

This is not liberal. Among the left, this is a remnant of the socialist approach that prioritizes group identity over individual autonomy. Among the right, it is ironically a throwback from the British colonial "divide and rule" approach. Classical liberalism focuses on individual autonomy. I refer here to liberalism as it is understood in the philosophical sense, not as it's understood in the United States to refer to the Democratic Party—that's a party-political usage. The great liberal betrayal of this generation is that in the name of liberalism, communal rights have been prioritized over individual autonomy within minority groups. And minorities within minorities really do suffer because of this betrayal. The people I really worry about when we have this conversation are feminist Muslims, gay Muslims, ex-Muslims—all the vulnerable and bullied individuals who are not just stigmatized but in many cases violently assaulted or killed merely for *being* against the norm.

This is why I don't like the "fellow-travelers" who would hold hands with extreme Islamists and walk along the path with them to entirely illiberal ends, believing they're doing Muslims a favor, when in fact they're surrendering all those Muslims who seek reform—to their deaths, in many instances—by quietly acquiescing to regimes and principles that would aspire to have them killed.

But there's another side to this, of which we must be careful. More so in Europe than in America, we have a serious problem with the rise of the right wing. In Greece, for example, the neo-Nazi party Golden Dawn has had political influence. In Britain we have had troubles with certain street movements. I was involved in helping Tommy Robinson leave the English Defence League because he saw that it was being infiltrated by neo-Nazis, and he didn't want anything to do with that. After he left the EDL, a new, smaller organization emerged, whose members started raiding mosques and handing out Bibles in broad daylight while dressed in military gear—which, as you can imagine, caused a lot of community tension. East Germany is facing acute problems with neo-Nazism.

So along with the "fellow-travelers"—and I've explained why I disagree with them—you have these bigots. Now, the bigots, whether they are of the Islamist variety or the anti-Muslim variety, essentially agree on a few matters. One is their belief that Islam itself—not Islamism—is a supremacist ideology that is here to take over the world; another is that, therefore, Muslims and non-Muslims can never live equally and peacefully together, but must separate into religiously defined entities.

Of course, you can see how that suits Islamists, but it also suits Golden Dawn and other groups that would be happy to expel all Muslims from Europe, even those who were born and raised there. These two groups share a vision, except that for one, it manifests—in its most extreme form—in the terrorist Anders Breivik, and for the other, in the 7/7 jihadist terrorists in London. I was not surprised to learn that Breivik quoted al-Qaeda extensively in his terrorist manifesto. One of these extremes is opposed to a "Muslim takeover," and the other is in favor of it, but they both subscribe to that divisive, sectarian apocalyptic vision. To counter such extremism, our challenge is to expose and undermine the "fellow-travelers," which I try to do on a regular basis, while at the same time opposing the bigots.

Harris I agree with everything you just said. I once wrote an article titled "The End of Liberalism?" in which I observed that these "fellow-travelers" have made it nearly impossible for well-intentioned, pluralistic, liberal people to speak honestly on this topic—leaving only fascists, neo-Nazis, and other right-wing lunatics to do the job. On some occasions the only people making accurate claims about the motivations of Islamists and jihadists are themselves dangerous bigots. That's terrifying. We have extremists playing both sides of the board in a clash of civilizations, and liberals won't speak sensibly about what's happening.

Nawaz Okay, because that latter part, the bigot part, isn't that controversial, I want to talk a bit longer about the "fellow-traveler" part, and why these people are reverse racists. It is because they come at this from the assumption that all Muslims think in a certain way, so any Muslim who doesn't think like that can't be a "real" or "authentic" Muslim. Now, what worse form of bigotry could you possibly adopt than the idea that all 1.6 billion people in the world who subscribe to a particular religious denomination must think and behave in the same way? This sounds like a right-wing approach, but the "fellow-travelers," or the regressive leftists, have adopted it. Allow me to elaborate.

If you're a Muslim liberal speaking as I do, challenging Islamism, the "fellow-travelers" somehow perceive you as being not a genuine conservative Muslim. The "fellow-travelers" then promote "real" voices as legitimate interlocutors, because they seek "purity" and "cultural authenticity" in their orientalist desire to maintain a group identity. So of course a downward spiral begins. The question becomes "Okay, what does being a Muslim mean?" This quickly degenerates into "Well, he's a purer Muslim—let's listen to him."

Such an approach inevitably ends up empowering fundamentalists as the most authentic, because of course the one who wins the game of "Who's a purer Muslim?" and outdoes others in a piety contest is the stubborn, dogmatic fundamentalist. This is how "fellow-travelers" disempower liberals and reformers. Without realizing it, they also adopt the role of thought police by asserting that liberalism isn't authentic to Muslims. Again, this is reverse bigotry kicking in.

I want those in what I call the regressive left who are reading this exchange to understand that the first stage in the empowerment of any minority community is the liberation of reformist voices within that community so that its members can take responsibility for themselves and overcome the first hurdle to genuine empowerment: the victimhood mentality. This is what the American civil rights movement achieved, by shifting the debate. Martin Luther King Jr. and other leaders took responsibility for their own communities and acted in a positive and empowering way, instead of constantly playing the victim card or rioting in the streets. Perpetuating this groupthink mind-set is both extremely dangerous and in fact disempowering.

Harris Yes, and the irony is that these liberals don't see that they've abandoned women, gays, freethinkers, public intellectuals, and other powerless people in the Muslim world to a cauldron of violence and intolerance. Rather than support the rights of women and girls to not live as slaves, for instance, Western liberals support the right of theocrats to treat their wives and daughters however they want—and to be spared offensive cartoons in the meantime.

Nawaz Now, as to the view that this is how anyone who had suffered imperialism or colonialism would behave: no, it's not. Entire countries such as India, were colonized. There's a difference between what's happening in Iraq with the so-called Islamic State's attempted genocide of the Yazidi community and how Gandhi acted in India. Let's take Iraq as a case study and think about it: What does killing the Yazidi population on Mount Sinjar have to do with US foreign policy? What does enforcing headscarves (tents, in fact) on women in Waziristan and Afghanistan, and lashing them, forcing men to grow beards under threat of a whip, chopping off hands, and so forth, have to do with US foreign policy?

Harris This catalogue of irrelevancy could be extended indefinitely. What does the Sunni bombing of Shia and Ahmadi mosques in Pakistan have to do with Israel or US foreign policy?

Nawaz Now, none of this means that there aren't problems in foreign policy. But we've all got to learn as a community, as a society, to be more nuanced in this debate. Earlier we mentioned the four factors in radicalization: a grievance narrative, whether real or perceived; an identity crisis; charismatic recruiters; and ideological dogma.

Where there is a genuine grievance, such as the genocide in Bosnia, it needs to be addressed. Where there's a perceived grievance, the perception must be encouraged to unravel. Addressing real or perceived grievances will stem the flow of angry young fifteen-year-olds before they are recruited. We can say, "Okay, I see why you're angry about Bosnia—but have you considered that the Americans intervened in the end and helped put a stop to it? Why don't they get some credit for that?"

Harris However, on the topic of perceived versus genuine grievances, religion plays a decidedly unhelpful role. For instance, what do you make of the fact that there are more protests in Muslim communities over Israel than over the Islamic State? Even more preposterous is the fact that if a pastor in Florida burns a copy of the Qur'an—or merely *threatens* to do so—it reliably produces more outrage in dozens of Muslim societies than the atrocities committed daily by Sunnis against Shia ever will.

Nawaz Yes, a peculiar trait of holding certain symbols as sacred and intimately tied to one's own identity is that they can often become more important than human life. No grievance, real or perceived, is ever seen except through the lens of dogma. Why is it, for example, that an Islamist will not be as moved by an atrocity committed by Muslims against non-Muslims, yet when Sunni Muslims are the perceived victims there is uproar? If we are truly concerned about human rights and injustice, we would be moved equally by all human rights crimes, and would act in a systematic way to deal with them as best we can. So I take the point you just made. What I would add is that dogma is a lens through which grievances are filtered.

Another factor worth mentioning at this stage, my second, is the identity crisis. It is very easy, even for non-Islamist Muslims, to become incredibly tribal in their interpretation of the above mentioned grievances. So, along with dogma, tribal identity leads many Muslims to speak out only in defense of "our" people, because that's the extent of any emotional energy we have. Either lens through which grievances are interpreted—dogma or tribalism—must be addressed head-on. I challenge both, because of course the grievances themselves will always be there. It's the nature of life. What we *can* change is the ideological lens, or the tribal nature of one's identity, or the identity-politics games we tend to play. I believe that indulging identity politics can be dangerous. It usually leads to division. It doesn't lead to communities' standing together.

Harris I agree. However, such tribalism is one of the consequences of religion. There are other sources of tribalism—nationalism and racism, for instance—but a shared religious identity has global reach. As I've said, it creates in-group loyalty and out-group hostility, even when members of one's own group are acting in abhorrent ways. Muslims often rally to the cause of other Muslims no matter how badly behaved they are, simply because they happen to be Muslim. Other groups do this as well, but it is especially a problem among Muslims in the twenty-first century.

The Nature of Islam

Harris You used the term "fundamentalist" earlier, and I want to clarify another point of possible confusion for our readers. In English, the term "fundamentalist" has been inherited from a specific strand of American Christianity. In that context, it means someone who believes in the divine origin and inerrancy of scripture. When we use this term with reference to Islam, we may lead people to believe that *mainstream* Muslims do not consider the Qur'an to be the literal word of the creator of the universe. I want to ask you about this, because my understanding is that basically all "moderate" Muslims—that is, those who aren't remotely like Islamists, or even especially conservative, in their social attitudes—are nevertheless fundamentalists by the Christian standard, because they believe the Qur'an to be the literal and inerrant word of God.

Nawaz I think we have to be careful to avoid two mistakes in our approach to this conversation. One would be taking a snapshot of the state of Islam and Muslims today and assuming that's how things always were and always will be. The other would be focusing explicitly on what we think the text says rather than on the method through which the text is approached, because I would argue that no approach to a text is without method—even what you would call literalism and what I call "vacuous literalism." (In fact, in many instances, some of which we will address, a purely literal interpretation leads to a surprisingly liberal outcome.) For me, vacuousness in itself is a method of approaching a text. I use the word "vacuous" because an insistence on ignoring apparent contradictions is not in keeping with *literal* wording. When you pick one passage of any text, and I demonstrate that it appears to contradict another passage, the insistence on being comfortable with those apparent contradictions and effectively arguing for both positions at the same time is a method. It doesn't make sense to me, but it's a method beyond mere literalism, as would be the method of attempting to reconcile such contradictions. Even agreeing on what the *literal* wording is requires a method.

Keeping those two points in mind, what would be my answer to your question? Well, to the first point, in Muslim history there have been people, known as the Mu'tazila, who didn't insist that the Qur'an was the eternal word of God. A modern-day advocate of this position is the Iranian Muslim philosopher and scholar AbdolKarim Soroush. The Mu'tazila became quite prominent until, as always, power determined which doctrine won. Usually this happens for political reasons, not because of the strength of the arguments. It happened at the Council of Nicaea, when Christianity was adopted by the Roman Empire, leading to its spread across much of Europe. Political decisions made by empires can determine and have determined which doctrines become orthodoxy. So it was with Islam.

Part of the history of Muslim "doctrine being shaped by power" lies in the story of the Muslim dispute over whether the Qur'an was created by God or is his eternal word. I refer to this dispute not to take one view or another—I won't take theological stances here—but to highlight the variety in traditional Islamic theology on questions such as this. Having the ruling doctrine at one stage, the Mu'tazila were eventually defeated by the Asha'ira, led by Imam Ash'ari, whose views on the eternal, uncreated nature of the Qur'an then became accepted as orthodoxy. Imam Ash'ari was, in fact, a defector from the Mu'tazila, which shows how popular the Mu'tazila view once was. This is why most Muslims today believe that the Qur'an is the eternal, literal word of God, despite neo-Mu'tazilite thinkers such as Soroush and others, who still make the opposite case.

So, my first point was that just because some-thing is the way it is today, that doesn't mean it's what it was yesterday or what it will be tomorrow. Because there is no clergy in Islam, these matters are constantly evolving. I'd argue that no doctrine on earth has ever been or will ever be immutable because of course doctrines are constructs— the work of human beings. I think this will always be the case. Again, I need to qualify this. I do not speak as somebody who holds himself up as a reli-gious leader or has a vested interest in resolving this particular theological dispute. My aim is merely to show just how closed the debate around Islam has become, whether the debaters are Muslims or even certain non-Muslims.

My role is to probe and ask skeptical questions about interpretive methodology, Muslim history, identity, politics, policy, values, and morality. But Dr. Usama Hasan, Quilliam's senior Islamic scholar and a religious imam, takes a position on reform theology. Dr. Hasan's positions are not Quilliam's official positions—Quilliam is a secular organization—but we will support the work of scholars such as Dr. Hasan as part of our role in showcasing variety in theology. I believe that this variety will lead us to secularism and liberalism.

Harris The tensions you've been describing are familiar to all religious moderates, but they seem especially onerous under Islam. The problem is that moderates of all faiths are committed to reinterpreting, or ignoring outright, the most dangerous and absurd parts of their scripture—and this commitment is precisely what makes them moderates. But it also requires some degree of intellectual dishonesty, because moderates can't acknowledge that their moderation comes from *outside* the faith. The doors leading out of the prison of scriptural literalism simply do not open from the inside. In the twenty-first century, the moderate's commitment to scientific rationality, human rights, gender equality, and every other modern value—values that, as you say, are potentially universal for human beings—comes from the past thousand years of human progress, much of which was accomplished in spite of religion, not because of it. So when moderates claim to find their modern, ethical commitments within scripture, it looks like an exercise in self-deception. The truth is that most of our modern values are *antithetical* to the specific teachings of Judaism, Christianity, and Islam. And where we do find these values expressed in our holy books, they are almost never *best* expressed there.

Moderates seem unwilling to grapple with the fact that all scriptures contain an extraordinary amount of stupidity and barbarism that can always be rediscovered and made holy anew by fundamentalists—and there's no principle of moderation *internal* to the faith that prevents this. These fundamentalist readings are, almost by definition, more complete and consistent—and, therefore, more honest. The fundamentalist picks up the book and says, "Okay, I'm just going to read every word of this and do my best to understand what God wants from me. I'll leave my personal biases completely out of it." Conversely, every moderate seems to believe that his interpretation and selective reading of scripture is more accurate than God's literal words. Presumably, God could have written these books any way He wanted. And if He wanted them to be understood in the spirit of twenty-first-century secular rationality, He could have left out all those bits about stoning people to death for adultery or witchcraft. It really isn't hard to write a book that prohibits sexual slavery—you just put in a few lines like "Don't take sex slaves!" and "When you fight a war and take prisoners, as you inevitably will, don't rape any of them!" And yet God couldn't seem to manage it. This is why the approach of a group like the Islamic State holds a certain intellectual appeal (which, admittedly, sounds strange to say) because the most straightforward reading of scripture suggests that Allah advises jihadists to take sex slaves from among the conquered, decapitate their enemies, and so forth.

Imagine that a literalist and a moderate have gone to a restaurant for lunch, and the menu promises "fresh lobster" as the specialty of the house. Loving lobster, the literalist simply places his order and waits. The moderate does likewise, but claims to be entirely comfortable with the idea that the lobster might not really be a lobster after all— perhaps it's a goose! And, whatever it is, it need not be "fresh" in any conventional sense—for the moderate understands that the meaning of this term shifts according to the context. This would be a very strange attitude to adopt toward lunch, but it is even stranger when considering the most important questions of existence—what to live for, what to die for, and what to kill for. Consequently, the appeal of literalism isn't difficult to see. Human beings reflexively demand it in almost every area of their lives. It seems to me that religious people, to

ISLAM AND THE FUTURE OF TOLERANCE

the extent that they're *certain* that their scripture was written or inspired by the Creator of the universe, demand it too.

So when you say that no religion is *intrinsically* peaceful or warlike, and that every scripture must be interpreted, I think you run into problems, because many of these texts aren't all that elastic. They aren't susceptible to just *any* interpretation, and they commit their adherents to specific beliefs and practices. You can't say, for instance, that Islam recommends eating bacon and drinking alcohol. And even if you could find some way of reading the Qur'an that would permit those things, you can't say that its *central* message is that a devout Muslim should consume as much bacon and alcohol as humanly possible. Nor can one say that the central message of Islam is pacifism. (However, one *can* say that about Jainism. All religions are not the same.) One simply cannot say that the central message of the Qur'an is respect for women as the moral and political equals of men. To the contrary, one can say that under Islam, the central message is that women are second-class citizens and the property of the men in their lives.

I want to be clear that when I used terms such as "pretense" and "intellectual dishonesty" when we

first met, I wasn't casting judgment on you personally. Simply living with the moderate's dilemma
may be the only way forward, because the alternative would be to radically edit these books. I'm not
such an idealist as to imagine that will happen. We
can't say, "Listen, you barbarians: These holy books
of yours are filled with murderous nonsense. In the
interests of getting you to behave like civilized
human beings, we're going to redact them and
give you back something that reads like Kahlil
Gibran. There you go . . . Don't you feel better
now that you no longer hate homosexuals?" However, that's really what one should be able to do in
any intellectual tradition in the twenty-first century.
Again, this problem confronts religious moderates
everywhere, but it's an excruciating problem for
Muslims.

Nawaz Yes, I'd agree with that last sentence. It's certainly an excruciating one for Muslims, because it's
currently, and I've said this openly, one of the
biggest challenges of our time—particularly in a
British and European context, as witnessed by the
sad and horrendous atrocities committed against
hostages in Syria by British and European Muslim
terrorists. We definitely have to acknowledge that

anything we say could apply to Judaism and Christianity. But a particular strand of a politicized version of the Muslim faith is causing a disproportionate share of problems in the world, so there are good reasons to focus on that strand. I don't dispute any of that.

Just as a side note, you say that in the twenty-first century we should have the right to edit any holy book, but of course there will always be value in preserving texts as they were, say, a thousand years ago, even as historical documents. I don't think the issue is the physical state of the texts we're looking at. This brings me neatly to everything else you said: I think the challenge lies with interpretation, the methodologies behind reform, whether reformists are in fact continuing a pretense, and whether this challenge is insurmountable. I think it's about approach.

Let's start with this: You're very clearly speaking from an intellectual perspective, you're trying to approach this consistently, you're trying to approach this with an understanding of the challenges ahead, and you're trying to be sensitive and not harm my work. I appreciate all that. But you also have to recognize that you're speaking from the luxury of living in—were probably born and raised in—a mature secular, democratic society. It can sometimes be very hard to make a mental leap and put yourself into the mind of the average Pakistani. I know many Pakistani atheists who—alongside liberal Muslims—are trying to democratize their society from within Pakistan. You and I can have this discussion without fear, but for them such open discussions can result in death.

Harris Of course. And I hear from many of these people. I'm well aware that millions of nominally Muslim freethinkers are in hiding out of necessity. This is one of the things I find so insufferable about the liberal backlash against critics of Islam— especially the pernicious meme "Islamophobia," by which anyone who thinks Islam merits special concern at this moment in history is branded a bigot. What worries me is that so many moderate Muslims believe that "Islamophobia" is a bigger problem than literalist Islam is. They seem more outraged that someone like me would equate jihad with holy war than that millions of their co-religionists do this and commit atrocities as a result.

In recent days, the Islamic State has been burning prisoners alive in cages and decapitating people by the dozen—and gleefully posting videos attesting to the enormity of their sadism online. Far from being their version of a My Lai massacre, these crimes against innocents represent what they *unabashedly stand for*. In fact, these ghastly videos have become a highly successful recruiting tool, inspiring young jihadists from all over the world to travel to Syria and Iraq to join the cause. No doubt, most Muslims are horrified by this, but the truth is that in the very week that the Islamic State was taking its barbarism to new heights, we saw a much larger outcry in the Muslim world over the killing of three college students in North Carolina, amid circumstances that made it very likely to have been an ordinary triple murder (as opposed to a hate crime indicating some wave of anti-Muslim bigotry in the US). This skewing of priorities produces a grotesque combination of political sensitivity and moral callousness—wherein hate crimes against Muslims in the US (which are tiny in number, often property-related, and still dwarfed fivefold by similar offenses against Jews)[12] appear to be of greater

---

12. And this was true even in 2002, in the immediate aftermath of the events of September 11, 2001; http://www.fbi.gov/stats-services/crimestats.

concern than the enslavement and obliteration of countless people throughout the Muslim world.

As you say, even having a conversation like this is considered a killing offense in many circles. I hear from Muslims who are afraid to tell their own parents that they have lost their faith in God, for fear of being murdered by them. These people say things like "If a liberal intellectual like you can't speak about the link between specific doctrines and violence without being defamed as a bigot, what hope is there for someone like me, who has to worry about being killed by her own family or village for merely expressing doubts about God?" So yes, I'm aware that one can't speak in Pakistan as I do here.

Nawaz This raises an intellectual point and a pragmatic point. Intellectually, I don't accept that there's a correct reading of scripture in essence. Now, you can point to many passages in the Qur'an and in *ahadith* (and I've certainly read them, because I memorized half the Qur'an while a political prisoner) that you would find very problematic, very concerning, and, on the face of it, very violent.

But, as I've said, to interpret any text, one must have a methodology, and in that methodology there are jurisprudential, linguistic, philosophical,

73

historical, and moral perspectives. Quentin Skinner, of the Cambridge School, wrote a seminal essay called "Meaning and Understanding in the History of Ideas."[13] This essay addresses the danger in assuming that there is ever a true reading of texts. It asks the question, does any piece of writing speak for itself? Or do we impose certain values and judgments on that text when interpreting it?

I personally do not use the term "literal" readings, because this implies that such readings are the *correct*, literal meaning of the texts. I would simply call it "vacuous." Similar to the printing press's influence on the Reformation, increased Internet access has facilitated a more patchwork, democratized, populist approach to interpreting Islamic texts. Now, the key for me (and this is only the intellectual point; I'll move to the pragmatic in a minute) is that if we accept that texts are, in fact, a bunch of ideas thrown together and arbitrarily called a "book," then nothing in a vacuous reading of a text makes it better than other interpretations. The question is, do we accept a vacuous approach

13. Q. Skinner, "Meaning and Understanding in the History of Ideas." *History and Theory* 8, no. 1 (1969): 3–53.

to reading scripture—picking a passage and saying this is its true meaning regardless of everything else around it—or do we concede that perhaps there are other methods of interpretation?

It comes down to our starting point: If one were to assume that a correct, unchanging reading of Islamic scripture never existed and that, from inception to now, it has always been in the spirit of its times, then the reform approach would be the intellectually consistent one. Indeed, we would expect it to be the majority view today. This approach stands in opposition to that of the very organized, vocal, and violent minority that has been shouting everyone else down. If, on the other hand, we start from the premise that the vacuous reading was the *original* approach to scripture, then the reform view stands little chance of success. There may be no answer here. I don't think this question has been resolved when it comes to interpreting the US Constitution, or Shakespeare, or indeed any religious scripture.

So, pragmatically speaking, what can be done? If somebody in Pakistan were to raise with me the issues you have raised, they could be killed. In such a stifling atmosphere, what is the solution? (I don't want our readers to think that all Muslim-majority countries are the same. For instance, in the middle of Ramadan 2014, Turkey witnessed a gay-pride march.)

A sensible way forward would be to establish this idea that there is no correct reading of scripture. This is especially easy for Sunnis—who represent 80 percent of the Muslims around the world— because they have no clergy. If a particular passage says "Smite their necks," to conclude, despite all the passages that came before it and everything that comes after it, that this passage means "Smite their necks today" is to engage in a certain method of interpretation. If we could popularize the understanding that all conclusions from scripture are but interpretations, then all variant readings of a holy book would become a matter of differing human perspectives.

That would radically reduce the stakes and undermine the claim that the Islamists are in possession of God's words. What is said in Arabic and Islamic terminology is: This is nothing but your *ijtihad*. This is nothing but your *interpretation* of the texts as a whole. There was a historical debate about whether or not the doors of *ijtihad* were closed. It concluded that they cannot be closed, because Sunni Muslims have no clergy. Anyone can interpret scripture if she is sufficiently learned in that scripture, which means that even extremists may interpret scripture. The best way to undermine extremists' insistence that truth is on their side is to argue that theirs is merely one way of looking at things. The only truth is that there is no correct way to interpret scripture.

When you open it up like that, you're effectively saying there is no right answer. And in the absence of a right answer, pluralism is the only option. And pluralism will lead to secularism, and to democracy, and to human rights. We must all focus on those values without worrying about whether atheism is the most intellectually pure approach. I genuinely believe that if we focus on the pluralistic nature of interpretation and on democracy, human rights, and secularism—*on these values*—we'll get to a time of peace and stability in Muslim-majority countries that then allows for conversations like this. Questioning whether God really exists would become a choice, open to all.

Currently, that focus is an impossible task in most Muslim-majority contexts. I'd also argue that we don't approach any other text, whether it be literature or anything else, with a deterministic understanding—

Harris Except that there are more and less plausible readings of any text.

Nawaz Yes, okay. I can't sit here and say to you that I've got a reading that justifies eating bacon. That's a very good example you gave. However, the civilizational challenge of our age isn't going to come down to eating bacon.

Harris I've known a few people who might disagree with you. But I take your point.

Nawaz There's another approach. Let's use bacon here to symbolize something bigger—an ability to move away from viewing religion as a set of legal injunctions. For example, in one tradition, the Prophet speaking in God's words narrated, "Oh, my people"—this is God addressing the believers—"If you don't sin and repent, I will bring a group of people more blessed than you who will sin and who do repent, because I want your repentance."

This and other passages like it led to a school within traditional Islamic thought that rejects any aspiration to human perfection or achieving utopia on earth. Indeed, many Sufi groups, including the Mulaamatiyya and the Qalandariyya, became quite keen in their right to sin. They argued that we're not angels walking on earth, and God is expecting repentance. What does that achieve? Rather than producing an interpretation that legalizes your symbolic bacon, it produces a "relationship with scripture" that looks at texts in a completely different way. It's no longer a matter of strict legal injunctions but a spiritual, mystical relationship with God, a journey.

These two methodologies, the view that *no text speaks for itself,* and our *relationship to scripture* being about spirituality more than legalese, do not require one to be a believer in God to concede the point.

Harris Well, that's all very interesting. I agree that finding a scriptural basis for liberally interpreting scripture will be indispensable. And the distinction you make between the intellectual problem and the pragmatic one is, in the context of this conversation, my primary concern. Despite what I said about the problems of religious moderation, I have no interest in debating you on the existence of God, or even on the legitimacy of believing that the Qur'an is the word of God. As I said, I want to support you, and I see your job as finding a way forward on the practical problem of reform.

However, I'm worried that progress on the practical problem will always be impeded by inertia on the intellectual one. Any position arrived at through this (granted, more appealing and more modern) approach to interpretation seems unstable, because fundamentalism can always rise again. And it will *tend* to rise again, to the degree that anyone feels the impulse to hew closely to the texts. What can you say to a person who thinks, "Okay, Maajid, you may be smarter than I am, but I just want to know what the Qur'an actually says. It says here that I should hate and fear infidels and take none as friends. So I'm just going to go with that and not split hairs."

There are many places in the Qur'an and *ahadith* where the most straightforward reading seems to yield something akin to the clear prohibition against eating bacon. Consider apostasy: Have you found a way to lift the stigma from this thought crime, or at least make it a nonpunishable offense?

Nawaz Yes, we've actually published a paper on that. I didn't write it. Dr. Hasan did. You saw his fatwa against the Islamic State on the front page of the *Sunday Times.*

Harris Yes, I did. I spread that on social media the moment I saw you had published it.

Nawaz Yes. So Dr. Hasan published a paper on the specific question of leaving the religion and freedom of belief.[14] Looking at the legal arguments specifically, this issue is slightly easier to address than your symbolic case of bacon. The criminalization of apostasy comes from a solitary *hadith* that appears to be inconsistent with other *ahadith* and even certain passages of the Qur'an. What do we do with that inconsistency? This is where one must enter into methodologies.

If somebody says, "Yes, but the *hadith* says this," it is for somebody like Dr. Hasan to say, "Yes, but the Qur'an says that." Now we have two sources saying different things. How can we reconcile them? How can we popularize a more considered

---

14. U. Hasan, "No Compulsion in Religion: Islam & the Freedom of Belief," Quilliam Foundation, 2013; http://www.quilliamfoundation.org/free-publications/.

approach, such as saying, "Let's put everything together and arrive at a more holistic understanding of what scripture might possibly say"? This requires organizing at the grass roots. Unless there exists a secular democratic equivalent of the Muslim Brotherhood—or of all the Islamist groups that have been working to popularize their approach since 1928—to teach the paper in study circles in Pakistan, in Egypt, in Syria, in Iraq, Dr. Hasan's writing will have no opportunity to make an impact. This level of organization, more than a desire to edit the Qur'an, is what's missing.

One of the things I have attempted in Pakistan is to help create such a movement: I helped to found Khudi, a grassroots social movement that seeks to popularize democratic culture there. We're attempting to do that not just because of the pragmatic necessity, but also because of our genuinely held belief in civil society activism as a means for change.

Harris No doubt you are right about the necessity of starting a social movement that champions reformist interpretations of scripture. But the contents of scripture still pose a problem. Often, when one attempts to reconcile contradictions between the Qur'an and *ahadith,* one is left to choose between edicts that are terrible (flogging adulterers) and those that are worse (stoning them). So a multiplicity of interpretations is no panacea if all options are bad.

It seems to me that the Qur'an contains two central messages, and I would be interested to hear you reflect on how they might be open to a reformist approach—because, as generally understood, they seem inimical to pluralism, secularism, and everything else you're espousing.

The first is the demonization of infidels. However I squint my eyes or cock my head, a hatred and fear of infidels seems central to the Qur'an. Muslims are told to have no friends among them and are assured that Allah will mock, curse, shame, and destroy them on the Day of Judgment. In fact, their very skins will testify to their misdeeds, and they will burn for eternity in hellfire. There's simply no question that, under Islam, being an infidel is considered the worst possible deviation from the good life. Again, this idea isn't foreign to other religions—Judaism and Christianity both have a version of it. The difference is in emphasis. The evil of unbelief is spelled out in the Qur'an on almost every page, and one finds only a few stray lines—for example, "There is no compulsion in religion"

(2:256)—with which to offset the general message of intolerance. There is also the doctrine of "abrogation," under which later—generally less tolerant—verses are believed to supersede earlier ones. My understanding is that 2:256 is nullified in this way.

The second central message—the other side of the same coin, really—is the promise of paradise, which explicitly devalues life in this world. Obviously, that isn't unique to Islam either, but the belief in martyrdom, and in jihad as a way of achieving it, is primarily a Muslim phenomenon. Islam teaches that dying in defense of the faith is among the surest paths to paradise—and the only one to reach it directly, bypassing the Day of Judgment. Some teachings suggest that a martyr can bring seventy of his dearest friends and family in after him. And we all know about the virgins who seem to guarantee that eternity will be spent in an open-air bordello. The belief that a life of eternal pleasure awaits martyrs after death explains why certain people can honestly chant, "We love death more than the infidels love life." Again, you and I both know that these people aren't bluffing. They truly believe in martyrdom—as evidenced by the fact that they regularly sacrifice their lives, or watch their children do so, without a qualm.

As we've been having this dialogue there was an especially horrific attack on a school in Peshawar, Pakistan, where members of the Taliban murdered 145 people, 132 of them children. The details are gruesome—and I don't intend to dwell on them—but it is important to understand the irrationality and horror that these numbers conceal. We are talking about a group of young men who were willing to burn a teacher alive in front of her pupils, butcher every child they could get their hands on, and then blow themselves up to maximize the carnage and avoid being captured. It is very difficult for most people to understand how this behavior could be possible, and they generally imagine that only madmen could act this way.

However, I've long been worried that a belief in paradise can lead ordinary people to perpetrate atrocities of this kind or condone the atrocities of others. For instance, here is an excerpt from an online conversation that Ali A. Rizvi had with a Taliban supporter in the aftermath of the massacre in Peshawar (translated from Urdu and annotated by Rizvi; the speaker is the Taliban supporter):[15]

---

15. A. A. Rizvi, personal communication.

"Human life" only has value among you worldly materialist thinkers. For us, this human life is only a tiny, meaningless fragment of our existence. Our real destination is the Hereafter. We don't just believe it exists, we know it does.

Death is not the end of life. It is the beginning of existence in a world much more beautiful than this. As you know, the [Urdu] word for death is "intiqaal." It means "transfer," not "end."

Paradise is for those of pure hearts. All children have pure hearts. They have not sinned yet . . . They have not yet been corrupted by [their kafir parents]. We did not end their lives. We gave them new ones in Paradise, where they will be loved more than you can imagine.

They will be rewarded for their martyrdom. After all, we also martyr ourselves with them. The last words they heard were the slogan of Takbeer ["Allah u Akbar"].

Allah Almighty says Himself in Surhah Al-Imran [3:169–170] that they are not dead.

You will never understand this. If your faith is pure, you will not mourn them, but celebrate their birth into Paradise.

I believe we should take declarations of this kind at face value—and understand that those who think this way pose a genuine danger to civilization. The problem, however, is that this way of thinking seems to be readily justified by recourse to scripture. On any list of Islamic doctrines in need of reform, I think those relating to infidels and to martyrdom should be at the very top.

Nawaz The questions you've raised are serious problems for Muslims to address in our age. I'm not in the business of denial, or of burying my head in the sand. That's why I do the work I do, because I want to confront these issues head-on. I wish other Muslims would confront them as well, and have conversations with the likes of you and Ayaan, because that's what's needed. It's how we will resolve all this. John Donvan, the commentator who moderated my Intelligence Squared debate with Ayaan, put a question to her the second time around, at the Richmond Forum: "Well, what relevance do you have in this debate? You're not even a Muslim. You're an apostate. So why would anyone take you seriously discussing Islam?" I interjected, "Actually, no, it's wrong of you to say that to Ayaan, because she does have a role in this conversation." We cannot disempower people who aren't Muslims from discussing this, because everyone—the whole human race—has to deal with the implications of our failure to fix this question. We Muslims must get used to the fact that people will criticize our religion, just as we criticize everyone else's religion for not being "true." Some people will choose to leave the faith, and we Muslims will need to come to terms with this, and to understand how to treat ex-Muslims not just with civility but with the utmost respect. Critiquing Islam, critiquing any idea, is not bigotry. "Islamophobia" is a troubled and inherently unhelpful term. Yes, hatred of Muslims by neo-Nazi-style groups does exist, and it is a form of cultural intolerance, but that must never be conflated with the free-speech right to critique Islam. Islam is, after all, an idea; we cannot expect its merits or demerits to be accepted if we cannot openly debate it. So I'm not one to try to avoid these issues. We have to address them head-on.

Another tragedy that occurred while we were locked in this dialogue was the terrible jihadist terrorist attack on the Charlie Hebdo offices in Paris, France. This attack brings to the fore the importance of distinguishing between critiquing an idea and inciting hate crime against a specific cultural grouping of people.

My view is that no idea is above scrutiny, and no people are beneath dignity. As Ali A. Rizvi points out, if I say "smoking is bad," this does not mean that I believe all smokers to be bad people.[16] Worrying about inciting racial hatred in cartoons is legitimate, so that no group is racially targeted. It is why we don't like anti-Semitic cartoons. This is entirely distinct from a "blasphemy" motivation for censorship, which aims to silence scrutiny of a powerful idea and its founder, inspiring to billions. We must not confuse these two different concerns. This is the core of what most of us, especially Muslims, must reflect on in the wake of the tragedy in France.

Now, let's take some specific examples: alcohol, apostasy, infidels, and paradise—let's look at each one in turn. Below I will focus on the *texts don't speak for themselves* part of my thesis. However, one could equally engage with these matters through the *relationship you have with the text*, which, as discussed above, views religion more as a spiritual journey, and less a set of legal injunctions.

---

16. http://www.huffingtonpost.com/ali-a-rizvi/an-atheist-mus lims-perspective-on-the-root-causes-of-islamist-jihadism -and-the-politics-of-islamophobia_b_3159286.html.

Let's start with alcohol, because everyone as-
sumes that all alcohol is absolutely prohibited for
all Muslims. In Arabic the word assumed to mean
alcohol is *khamr*. There's a long-standing historical
discussion about what *khamr* means and whether
or not it's prohibited. An extremely early *tafsir* (exe-
gesis) of the Qur'an was by Imam Abu Bakr al-Jasas,
who hailed from the Hanafi school of jurisprudence
within the Sunni denomination of Islam. The
Hanafi school is known to be the first school of
interpretation and therefore the closest in prox-
imity to the time of the Prophet. In his interpretation of the Qur'an, al-Jasas discusses the linguistic
meaning of *khamr* at length and elaborates on why
for Hanafis a literal interpretation of the word
covers only a prohibition on wine from grapes. This
means that for the jurists of this first school, it was
permitted—and still is for those who follow the
early Hanafis—to consume any form of alcohol
other than wine. Among the Hanafis, this view is
ascribed to Abu Ja'far al-Tahawi, who in turn as-
cribes it directly to the founder of the Hanafi school,
Abu Hanifah, and his two students Abu Yusuf
and Muhammad. Once again, *and I cannot be
too careful here*, I mention this without prejudice,

not to favor this view but merely to demonstrate the surprisingly flexible way in which traditional jurists with clout were able to interpret the Qur'an, and to shed light on some methodological approaches that have been lost to most of us today.

In fact, by refusing to budge from the linguistic, *literal* meaning of *khamr*, and by refusing to apply its prohibition to anything but grape wine, these early Hanafis were making an extremely literalist yet nonvacuous argument. This is why I said earlier that in interpreting scripture there's a jurisprudential methodology and also a linguistic methodology.

The Hanafi school was strong in its linguistic approach to interpreting Arabic scripture. This reinforces a point made by Quentin Skinner: One cannot approach scripture by imposing upon it meanings that words have come to acquire today while ignoring what they meant then.

The argument carries on. There's a doctrine called *qiyas* in Islamic interpretation, which means "juristic analogy." Jurists after the Hanafis said: Yes, we can see that *khamr* meant only wine, but by *qiyas*—by analogy—we can say that intoxication was actually the reason behind the prohibition on wine. From this other jurists drew an analogy, thereby prohibiting all other alcoholic substances. Notice that these jurists conceded the point that *khamr* did originally mean grape wine only. The Hanafis responded by asking, well, if that was the case, why would the Prophet's companions be drinking other fermented drinks? No *qiyas* is valid if it contradicts specific evidence, and the actions of the Prophet's companions are specific evidence. Other jurists rebutted this by arguing that the actions of individual companions do not carry divine authority in their methodological approach, and so on and so forth.

Harris So you're saying that this same dexterity can be applied to the topics of unbelief and martyrdom?

Nawaz Yes, absolutely. That's but one example. I went into some depth with it merely to demonstrate the importance that interpretive methodologies played historically in reading Islamic scripture. Some Hanafis took a similar view regarding apostasy. The *hadith* you referred to is a solitary (*ahad*) *hadith*: "Whoever changes his persuasion (*din*), kill him." Some Hanafis argue that this couldn't possibly mean "kill apostates," because the *hadith* literally says "changes," which would imply entering as well as leaving Islam. The *hadith* doesn't literally say "kill whoever leaves Islam to follow any other religion." The issue arises here with the synonymous meanings for the Arabic word *din* (persuasion or religion). That's why some jurists took the view that this *hadith* cannot possibly be addressing apostasy.

This group of jurists then put this solitary *hadith* into context with the Qur'an and took the view that it contradicts the explicit prohibition against forced conversions: "There is no compulsion in religion." Therefore *din* could not have been intended to mean "religion" in the *hadith*. It may instead have been referring to changing persuasion to a political order—in other words, treason. This was evidenced by the example of the first caliph, Abu Bakr, who immediately after the Prophet's death fought in the Wars of "Apostasy," otherwise known as the Wars of Rebellion, against treacherous tribes. Some Hanafis argued that this solitary *hadith* was really addressing the obligation to fight those who attempt military insurrection from within an existing authority, or the obligation of citizens to fight in a civil war context. Of course, I'm not arguing that all Hanafi jurisprudence be held up today as a model of virtue. Much of it is rooted in medievalism. Rather, I'm merely attempting to demonstrate the nature of textual variance.

Let us take this *texts don't speak for themselves* approach and apply it to another fundamental principle of dogma that would appear intractable, and certainly incompatible with democratic society: the Islamist (not traditional Muslim) belief in the necessity of "ruling by Islam." To fully dissect how such a construct is partly a modern byproduct of the advent of the European nation state would require an essay in itself. However, Islamists do refer to certain plausible scriptural justifications in support of this tenet, which must be addressed. Qur'anic passages such as "the rule (*hukm*) is for none but God" and "whomsoever does not rule (*yahkum*) by what God has revealed, they are disbelievers" are among the most oft quoted in this regard.

Again, in applying a linguistic methodology, one learns of a dispute here as to whether the Arabic word used in these passages, *hukm*, means in its original usage "to rule" or "to judge." This subtle distinction in language makes all the difference. Of course, "to rule" may imply an active obligation to "implement" Islam as a "law" over society.

To judge is a more passive requirement to arbitrate using God's commands between those who voluntarily come to you seeking such arbitration, rather than actively seeking to "rule" over people. In this way the linguistic dispute here over the *literal* meaning of these passages becomes hugely significant.

Moreover, Islamists who would insist today that a version of *shari'ah* must be synchronized with law are vulnerable to the charge that the vast majority of *shari'ah* guidance—apart from the handful of injunctions related to the penal code (*hudud*)—carry with them no worldly criminal sanction for their violation. Thus, it has been argued that even if one were to take the view that Muslims must "rule" by God's revelation, that very same revelation does not stipulate criminal sanction—hence not mandating illegality—for almost all of what it deems religiously impermissible (*haram*). In fact, by stipulating criminal sanction for only a handful of penal codes (*hudud*)—including the amputation of the hand for theft, and so on—the text can be said to imply that all other religiously impermissible (*haram*) acts, which are the vast majority, are not subject to any fixed criminal law whatsoever, and therefore may remain legal, even while being *haram.*

Of course, this only leaves the matter of the penal codes (*hudud*) themselves, which Islamic jurists in the Ottoman empire did away with by utilizing Imam al-Shatibi's doctrine of "aims of Shari'ah" (*maqasid al-shari'ah*), which I shall return to below.[17]

In this way the sacred and the secular can be delineated, and Islamists critiqued, without the need to exit significantly from existing Islamic tradition. The mere possibility of interpreting scripture in this way fundamentally undermines the Islamist insistence that only *they* speak in God's name, and only *they* are agents of His will.

It's the same with the question of cohabiting with "infidels." The Arabic word *kafir* is commonly translated to a word derived from Christianity, "infidel." There's a reason why jihadist movements weren't really popular before the nineteenth-century Islamist movements. For long periods of time, Muslims were relatively progressive. Of course they were living by very medieval standards

---

17. http://faith-matters.org/images/stories/fm-publications/the-tanzimat-final-web.pdf

that today we would find repugnant. But by comparison with other societies *at that time*, they were relatively—I say *relatively*—progressive, encouraging science and math. That is well documented.

So why didn't we have comparable problems relating to cohabiting with "infidels" within their societies? Because these debates had already been held. But modern-day Islamists, with their particularly vacuous approach to interpretation, have resurrected some of them. In the theological sphere, there's a well-known Muslim exegete, philosopher, and mystic, Ibn 'Arabi. He proposed a theory that eventually came to be known as *wahdat al-wujud*, or the "unity of being," which focused on a universal approach to oneness, truth, and justice in matters theological, regardless of one's religious heritage. Some followers of Imam al-Ash'ari, whom we mentioned earlier, also took the view that only those who—like Satan—recognize Islam as true and then knowingly reject it out of arrogance can be described as *kuffar*, or infidels. They referred to the *literal* Arabic meaning of the word *kafir*, "one who conceals," to argue that concealing the truth is a deliberate act and cannot be ascribed to anyone who doesn't recognize it as truth in the first instance. A related theory by Imam al-Shatibi, known as *maqasid al-shari'ah,* or the "aims of Shari'ah," again focuses on values and not dogma, this time in matters jurisprudential regardless of one's theological heritage. It transpires from these theological and scriptural theories that what matters are the values one holds, not the scripture one claims to derive them from. In your introductory remarks you suggested that if such universal values exist outside scripture, they can be equally applied to other scriptures—in which case it's not necessarily scripture that gives rise to these values, so what's the point of it? I think it's important to recognize the human tendency toward reverence and the role spirituality may play, as well as the evolutionary role played by religion. However, I personally prefer to focus on people's values, not the religious heritage they claim as the source of those values.

Harris I'm very happy to hear about these interpretive resources, but I have to offer a brief demurral to what sounds like an overly cheerful account of Islamic history. Most of human history is a bloodbath, of course, so Islam is not unique in this. But it is misleading to suggest that the problems of

Muslim triumphalism and intolerance are modern ones. I know that modern Islamism learned a trick or two from European fascism, but when Muslim armies were stopped at the gates of Vienna in 1683, the world had witnessed a thousand years of jihad—which had spread the faith from Portugal to the Caucasus to India to sub-Saharan Africa. Islam was spread primarily by conquest, not conversation. Infidels were forced to convert or die. "People of the book"—Jews and Christians—were given the option of paying a protection tax (*jizya*) and living in an apartheid state (as *dhimmi*). In fact, Muslim historians recorded in assiduous detail the numbers of infidels they slaughtered or enslaved and deported.[18]

It seems to me that a politically correct mythology is replacing history on many of these topics. Consider the Crusades. The Christians are often depicted as barbarian aggressors and the Muslims as their highly cultured victims. But the Crusades were primarily a *response* to 300 years of jihad (whether the crusaders were aware of the Islamic doctrine or not). They were a reaction to Muslim

---

18. Some of this material has been gathered in Andrew Bostom's book *The Legacy of Jihad.*

incursions in Europe, the persecution of Eastern Christians, and the desecration of Christian holy sites. And few people seem to remember that the crusaders *lost* all but the first of those wars.

Although the Crusades were undoubtedly an expression of religious tribalism, the idea of holy war is a late, peripheral, and in many ways self-contradictory development within Christianity— and one that has almost no connection to the life and teachings of Jesus. One can't say the same about the status of jihad under Islam.

Likewise, the vaunted peace of Andalusia is largely a fairy tale, first presented in the novels of Sir Walter Scott, Benjamin Disraeli, and others who romanticized Muslim civilization at its height. Apart from the experience of a few courtiers and poets, if life was ever good for Jews living under Muslim rule, it was good only by comparison with the most murderous periods of medieval Christendom. We can make such comparisons, as you point out, but the general reality was of a world absolutely suffocated by religious stupidity and violence.

Please don't misunderstand me. I'm not painting the West as blameless. It has much to atone for from the age of imperialism onward—especially the practice of slavery. But as you know, Muslims, too, practiced slavery in Africa, and Western slavers appear to have learned a good deal from them. In fact, Muslims regularly enslaved white Christian Europeans. For hundreds of years, to live or travel anywhere on the Mediterranean was to risk being captured by Barbary pirates and sold into slavery. It is believed that more than a million Europeans were enslaved and forced to work in North Africa by Muslims between the sixteenth and eighteenth centuries.

I don't think anything of substance turns on this history, because we have to deal with the world as we find it today. But I reject the idea that jihad and a hatred of infidels are modern phenomena. As you know, many people make this claim because they want to hold the West and Israel responsible for all the violence we see in the Muslim world—even, somehow, for the internecine conflict between Sunni and Shia. But the problem we must grapple with—and must inspire millions of others to grapple with—is that, whatever other historical and political factors are involved, the reality of martyrdom and the sanctity of armed jihad are about as controversial under Islam as is the resurrection of Jesus under Christianity. It is not an accident that millions of

Muslims recite the *shahadah* or make pilgrimage to Mecca. Neither is it an accident that in the year 2015, horrific footage of infidels and apostates being decapitated has become a popular form of pornography throughout the Muslim world. All these practices, including this ghastly method of murder, find explicit support in scripture.

Finding the Way Forward

Nawaz Your words about history are not incorrect, but I believe they are incomplete. My point was not to deny or excuse the barbarity that occurred throughout the medieval era. I am not interested in playing the blame game by arguing about what came first, jihad or Christian conquest. Throughout history most empires used a form of religion to conquer and plunder. Islam evolved in part as an imperialist cause. Aspects of it were bred of the presumptions of late-antique imperialism. The dream of a universal caliphate is a version of late Roman fantasies of a universal Christian empire. Frankly though, that's less relevant here. I am certainly not trying to blame the West or Israel for the rise of modern Islamism and jihadism—though it would be patently ridiculous to say that colonialism played no role whatsoever. I bring up the history simply to highlight a *relative* point. Islamist and jihadist refusal to cohabit with non-Muslims is *relatively* worse today than in the past. Witness the Islamic State's desire in Iraq to slaughter Yazidi men and enslave their women wholesale because they do not fit a narrow definition of "people of the book." However, the area known today as Iraq has been Muslim-majority for centuries; India, too, was ruled by Muslims for centuries. Yet in the former, Christians and Yazidis remained a minority without wholesale slaughter, and in the latter, Hindus remained a majority. This jihadist inability to reconcile anyone but Jews and Christians as protected people (if that) is a modern twist on our worst medieval prejudices.

Ibn 'Arabi's theories, and the view of followers of Imam al-Ash'ari that only malicious, arrogant rejection was deserving of the label *kafir*, practically do away with the concept of infidel, to be honest. I'm arguing that these debates were mostly settled. But they've been revived for various ideological, socioeconomic, and postcolonial reasons.

Let's take your second central message of the Qur'an, paradise. I have every respect for Ali A.

Rizvi; I personally enjoy his keen mind and scrupulously logical approach. The quotation from the Taliban supporter he translates that you cite above is in fact a perfect illustration of the vacuous certainty in one's approach to religion that I aim to highlight. Our antidote to such hellish certainty cannot be to similarly concur with certainty that his is the only correct approach to the concept of paradise, hell, and sending people there.

One of the most prolific and (in)famous jurists, whose ancient writings are held responsible for the revival of Wahhabism today, is Ibn Taymiyyah. Ibn Taymiyyah's best student, Ibn al-Qayyim al-Jawziyyah, took the idea of paradise and hell and looked at it and thought, hold on: one belief we have is the concept of an infinitely merciful God, and another is the possibility of infinite punishment in hell. But how can God be both infinitely merciful and infinitely vengeful? That doesn't make sense. Ibn al-Qayyim therefore took the view that hell is not really eternal. He focused in particular on passages in the Qur'an, after God's description of "eternal" hellfire, where caveats such as "except as God wills" and "everything terminates except His grace" appear.

Now, again, I don't want to get into the validity of any of these approaches, forever cherry-picking the so-called moderate view on every problematic text you give me. Any given subject has multiple interpretations, which demonstrates that there's no *correct* one. If we can understand that, then we arrive at a respect for difference, which leads to tolerance and then pluralism, which in turn leads to democracy, secularism, and human rights. This is the approach we should take with religion generally. Of course, this approach only works if our adversaries are prepared to talk. Those terrorist groups that wish to willfully target and slaughter children en masse in order to "send them to paradise" should face the full force of our global, civilizational consensus, and be crushed.

Harris Right. Well, I'm encouraged by that, although I'm often *dis*couraged when I actually look at the details. For instance, you mentioned the fatwa against the Islamic State that was signed by several British imams, which we both spread on social media. Obviously, I find this sort of effort praiseworthy. But what struck me about it was how tenuous its basis in Islamic doctrine seems. It comes down to honoring covenants and treaties—a duty that I can't imagine any serious Muslim believes will trump the obligation to defend the faith. The fatwa also cites the Mughals and the Ottomans as historical precedents for tolerance in the House of Islam. Apart from my aforementioned concerns about getting the history wrong—the Ottomans, for instance, perpetrated a genocide against Christians (Armenian, Assyrian, and Greek), killing millions— I mainly worry that such a precedent, where true, can't be nearly as persuasive as the example set by Muhammad himself—which, as you know, offers ample justification for religious violence.

So this fatwa, while better than no fatwa at all, is symptomatic of the problem I've been describing. Reformists either rely on examples that are not doctrinal—that is, instances in which Muslims behaved better than their scripture mandates—or cite something like a commitment to honoring covenants and treaties, which occasionally has sinister implications. One regularly hears Muslims saying, "Yes, we must follow the laws of England because our faith tells us that we should follow covenants." But many of these people want the laws to *change*— indeed, many want *shari'ah* established in the UK. Hand-waving displays of tolerance often conceal some very ugly truths—which puts one in mind of the doctrine of *taqqiya*, wherein it is said that Muslims are encouraged to lie to infidels whenever it serves their purpose. I hope you will enlighten me about that. But before you do, I'll give you another example, from a non-Muslim context, to show you how weird these conversations with the devout can sometimes be.

I once attended a wedding where I was introduced to a close friend of the groom. As it turned out, this man was an Orthodox Jew. After a suitable period of small talk, I said, "What's your opinion of all the barbarism in Leviticus, Deuteronomy, and Exodus? For instance, what do you make of that bit about a woman's not being a virgin on her wedding night—should we really take her to her father's doorstep and stone her to death?[19] Seems a bit harsh. And I rather like this woman our friend is marrying."

My companion then began to wax rabbinical on how these *seemingly* brutal strictures must be understood in the context of their time. Needless to say, he assured me that they don't apply today. In fact, he said, these rules applied only when there

---

19. Deuteronomy 22:13–21.

was a Sanhedrin—a supreme religious council that hasn't existed since the time of the Romans.

"Okay," I said, "so what happens when the Messiah comes back, as you surely expect he will, and you reconvene the Sanhedrin? Then what?"

Here I glimpsed the rueful smile of the cornered theocrat. "Well, that's a very interesting question," he said—to which he had no interesting or even sane answer. He simply conceded that if the Messiah came back and reconvened the Sanhedrin, well, then, yes—though mere mortals like ourselves might not see the wisdom of it—homosexuals, adulteresses, witches, and Sabbath breakers would be killed, and every other barbaric prescription found in the Old Testament would apply.

As I was contemplating where on his person I should aim my vomit, he managed this final defense of his religion: "You just don't understand what an obscenity—what a *sacrilege*—these things would represent in the presence of the Messiah and in the view of a properly consecrated Sanhedrin." Indeed, I don't.

Encounters of this kind make me want to know exactly what is behind carefully worded statements. And my fear is that when you have a fatwa like the one we circulated, pegged to covenants and trea-

ties, the serpent of theocracy may be hiding somewhere in the shadows. I worry that if things were
to change, and we had a Muslim-majority government, all pretense of tolerance would disappear and
we'd be on a swift ride back to the seventh century.

Nawaz Yes, that is a valid fear. My organization has a
track record of being consistent—not just in Britain,
where I was born and raised, but also in Pakistan
and other Muslim-majority countries. We take the
unequivocal view that no place on earth should
seek to impose any given interpretation of religion
over the rest of society.

The *taqqiya* that you referred to is a Shia concept. It doesn't apply to 80 percent of the world's
Muslims, who are Sunni. It's actually an intrafaith
concept that the Shia developed because they were
being persecuted by Sunnis. And sadly, today in
Pakistan they are being persecuted again. There
is no analogous Sunni doctrine. The only time
Sunnis seek to lie is when they're at war or under
duress. Besides, every nation uses war propaganda.
But that's a different discussion.

Harris I suspect that any Sunni jihadist or Islamist
could justify his deception by claiming to be on a

war footing with all infidels, so the point is probably moot.

Nawaz It's irrelevant because I could be doing *taqqiya* now in my explanation of what *taqqiya* is. What's important is that credible interlocutors have these sorts of conversations with you, with Ayaan, and with others, because when you trust someone, it's a lot easier to listen to what he's saying, regardless of whether *taqqiya* is a Sunni or a Shia concept. Such relationships can come only with hard work and seeing that we have everyone's best interests at heart.

As for the fatwa, it wasn't evidenced in terms of scripture because it was written very deliberately to make front-page headlines in the press, which it did. You can imagine that an overly theological document would not get onto the front page of London's *Sunday Times*. I would encourage you to read other papers by Dr. Hasan. He has written a paper on citizenship and reconciling the concept of the medieval form of the *dhimma*, when a head tax was levied on "people of the book."[20] He has

---

20. U. Hasan, *From Dhimmitude to Democracy: Islamic Law, Non-Muslims and Equal Citizenship*, Islamic Reform Series 3 (London: Quilliam, 2015).

used theological reasoning to develop the idea of *dhimma* into the modern context of citizenship.

The fatwa itself didn't go into much detail, but a lot of substantial work is being done in the background concerning many of these ideas. The whole idea of obeying your covenants and being responsible citizens within the British or the European context rests on the research for that longer paper of Dr. Hasan's.

When Dr. Hasan refers in the fatwa to the Ottomans and the Mughals, he is invoking a well-established doctrine to which all jurisprudential schools of thought within Sunni and Shia Islam agree, known as *ijma'a*, or the consensus of Muslims. That all Muslim-majority societies have joined the United Nations is an example of *ijma'a*. It can be invoked to say that Muslims are bound by the commitments they've made to the UN to respect human rights and so forth.

I do think the fatwa has three very specific benefits. One is something you've already mentioned, and that's the pragmatic recognition that a fatwa is better than no fatwa, because otherwise young would-be recruits to the Islamic State would read the silence of Islamic scholars as a form of consent to the heinous crimes of that group. A fatwa condemning the Islamic State is better than no fatwa.

Also, I made a point when I encouraged Dr. Hasan to embark upon this task. I advised him that the fatwa could not merely condemn. I think you circulated an interview on CNN in which I mentioned that I don't deserve thanks from you or anyone else for saying that you don't deserve to die. That's how low our bar has sunk. We've become happy to hear a Muslim condemning the Islamic State, yet even al-Qaeda condemns them. Condemning the Islamic State should not be the definition of a "moderate." So I advised Dr. Hasan that the fatwa should go further and place an active responsibility on Muslims to challenge the ideology behind the Islamic State, as part of our civic duty to condemn evil. I argued that Muslims are now duty bound to challenge this whole idea of imposing Islam on others, because it's not just hurting non-Muslims, it's hurting Islam and Muslims as well. The fatwa reflected this view.

The second benefit is that it provides an escape clause for somebody who sets out to do something irresponsible but has last-minute doubts. Let's keep in mind that we're speaking about people for whom secular, humanistic language simply does not resonate. These people think only in religious terms, and you know this because of your conversations with Orthodox Jewish rabbis and others. To believe that you're going to blow up everyone around you and go straight to paradise on a one-way ticket requires 100 percent certainty. If we can seed even 1 percent doubt, we may stop that suicide bomber.

The third benefit is that the fatwa reassures the mainstream. There are others in society who look at Muslims today and think: Why aren't you condemning the Islamic State? Why did you so vocally condemn Gaza but you don't condemn the Islamic State? Do you secretly sympathize with its members?

Harris I completely agree, and we need fatwas by the thousands on that front. Another thing I think we should discuss is the tension between honestly confronting the problems of conservative Islam, Islamism, and jihadism and feeding the narrative that "the West is at war with Islam." I admit that I have often contributed to this narrative myself, and rather explicitly. Of course, whenever I worry out loud about "the problem of Islam," I'm talking about a more or less literal (you would say "vacuous") reading of the Qur'an and *ahadith*. And

I'm careful to say that we are not at war with all (or even most) Muslims. But it seems to me that no matter how carefully one speaks on this issue, there is a problem of Muslim perception that keeps arising on the basis of two factors that we've already discussed. The first is the problem of identity: many Muslims feel a reflexive (and religiously mandated) solidarity with other Muslims, no matter how barbaric their commitments, simply because they happen to be Muslim. The second is the problem of ideology: scripture, read in anything but the most acrobatic, reformist way, seems to be on the side of the barbarians.

As a result of these two factors, we find that any action we take against jihadists—bombing the Islamic State, killing Osama bin Laden, and so on—seems to increase recruitment for extremist organizations and a more generalized anger toward the West. No matter how surgical or well-intended our actions, some number of Muslims will conclude that they must now defend their faith against infidel aggressors rather than recognize that groups like the Islamic State and al-Qaeda are the common enemies of all humanity. Again, their inability to recognize this appears to come from those two factors: it is taboo for a Muslim to side with non-Muslims who are killing or subjugating their "Muslim brothers and sisters"; and groups like the Islamic State and al-Qaeda are enacting very literal (and therefore plausible) interpretations of Islamic doctrine. Needless to say, there is also the vexing problem of collateral damage, which inevitably produces enemies, for reasons that are perfectly understandable.

In light of this, I'm wondering what you recommend we do to contain and (hopefully) eradicate the growing phenomenon of global jihad, and to marginalize Islamists and conservatives politically and culturally. No doubt we should seek to partner with Muslim states wherever possible when taking military action. But in cases where no partners are available, how should we proceed?

Nawaz I appreciate your recognition that your wording has often contributed to this "clash of civilizations" narrative. It is the nature of many people that they tend to hear only what they already *expect* to hear from any given speaker. They cease listening to the words of the speaker and instead react to what they have been *expecting* the speaker to say. This happens to me all the time, and I believe this has happened to you a few times too. In your defense, this is not always avoidable, but we are duty bound to try and minimize it through careful wording, so thank you.

You are correct that Muslim tribalism and vacuous literalism combined lend themselves to a generally hostile approach to "the other." This has been encouraged by many years of Islamist polarization, which in turn was built atop decades of leftist hostility toward America under Arab socialist (*Ba'thist*) regimes that politically identified with the Soviet Union.

A complete overhaul of cultural identity patterns and a reformed scriptural approach is required. Identity must start with humanity as a founding principle, and human rights as a basis. "My people" do not simply include any Muslim, no matter how barbaric. "My people" are human beings, and then those who share my multiple cultural references and human rights values, regardless of ethnicity, gender, sexuality, and religion. Beyond that, "my people" are those who simply share the land that I call my home, my neighbors. The Islamic concept of *ummah*, or people, must be reappraised here. Most Muslims today would view the *ummah* as comprising of solely other Muslims. This is where tribalism can emerge. However, again by taking a more adaptive look at texts, one can find that the

Prophet was reported to have included non-Muslims in his definition of *ummah* upon authoring a document—known as the Covenant of Medina—that regulated the rights and duties of those residing under his authority. Dr. Hasan's pamphlet exploring the nature of citizenship, *ummah*, and Muslim and non-Muslim cohabitation will be useful here.

Such scriptural reform must involve denying those who approach texts vacuously—albeit plausibly—from absolute certainty that theirs is the correct view, as I attempt to do in our dialogue above.

Moving on to the Islamic State, this scourge must be militarily and culturally defeated. Nothing but total defeat will suffice for a group that is so certain that it speaks for God. The Islamic State being able to claim victory against the entire world order is their biggest recruitment sergeant. It "proves" that God is on their side against all the odds. Defeat will demonstrate to the world's Muslims that the Islamic State speaks for nothing but medieval depravity. A military defeat will be but a short-term success. It must be coupled with a cultural defeat of what they stand for. But this is the hard part, for the Islamic State has not emerged from a vacuum.

For decades the Islamist ideology has been festering in the grass roots of Muslim political activism. It would have been impossible for the Islamic State to emerge if Islamism had not settled as the default form of political expression for many young Muslims around the world. This is why merely condemning the Islamic State, or defeating them militarily, is entirely insufficient. Similarly, this is why previously focusing on al-Qaeda's military defeat has also proven to be insufficient. The US killed bin Laden, yes, but something worse (which we couldn't have imagined prior to al-Qaeda) emerged to replace him. This will keep happening until and unless the ideology that breeds these groups is discredited. Islamism must be defeated.

The last two years of George W. Bush's term witnessed a basic recognition of this simple truth. But as with all democratic handovers, Barack Obama's team wanted nothing to do with the previous collective wisdom, including where Bush's team had learned from their many terrible mistakes. If the first few years of the Bush administration could be caricatured as an attempt at imposing values at the barrel of a gun, then President Obama's administration ditched the values and kept the gun.

Launching more drone strikes than Bush ever did and compiling a secret "kill list," President Obama's administration took the view that al-Qaeda was like an organized crime gang—disrupt the hierarchy, destroy the gang. Theirs was a concerted and dogmatic attempt at pretending that al-Qaeda was nothing but a fringe criminal group, and not a concrete realization of an ideological phenomenon with grassroots sympathy. They took this view in part because of how successful Islamist "fellow-traveler" lobbies had been in influencing Obama's campaign after the mistakes of the Bush years. For Islamists and their allies, the problem was "al-Qaeda inspired extremism," and not the extremism that had inspired al-Qaeda. Such an approach left us here at Quilliam incredibly frustrated. We gave many interviews and published many papers calling out the rise of this ideology for what it was: a full-blown jihadist insurgency.

This fundamental misdiagnosis and the US government's failure to recognize the jihadist insurgency led to jihadist groups metastasizing as the ideology continued to grow entirely unchecked. Recently, and only after the Islamic State's lightning successes in Iraq, did President Obama come to recognize the role ideology plays, and again this was in his last two years. Yet, in an almost comical twist that I have come to label the *Voldemort effect*,[21] as of the time of this dialogue, President Obama still cannot bring himself to *name* this ideology.

The *Voldemort effect* in this context entails not naming Islamism, nor distinguishing it from the multifaceted religion. By highlighting the need to "tackle the Islamic State's ideology" but refusing to name it, President Obama only increased the public's fear and made it easier for Muslimphobes, who will naturally assume the ideology Obama refers to is "Islam," to blame all Muslims.

As we have discussed, however, Islam is just a religion. *Islamism* is the ideology that seeks to impose any version of Islam over society. Islamism is, therefore, theocratic extremism. Jihadism is the use of force to spread Islamism. Jihadist terrorism is the use of force that targets civilians to spread Islamism. The Islamic State is merely *one* jihadist terrorist group. The problem was never "al-Qaeda-inspired"

---

21. Voldemort is the villain in J. K. Rowling's *Harry Potter* novels. The other characters in this story are so petrified of Voldemort that they refer to him as "He Who Must Not Be Named." Only a few diehards are prepared to call Voldemort by his actual name.

extremism, because extremism itself inspired al-Qaeda, and then inspired the Islamic State. It is this extremism that must be named—as Islamism—and opposed.

It is true that one cannot argue that the Islamic State represents all of Islam, just like one cannot argue that it has *nothing* to do with Islam. But it should be obvious that "a desire to impose Islam" cannot reasonably be said to have "nothing to do with Islam." Clearly, it has *something* to do with it. One may disagree with the Islamic State's interpretation of the faith, but imagine that we were debating its supporters: Would we be debating *Das Kapital* or Islamic scripture?

We must name the ideology behind the Islamic State so that we can refute it. It is crucial to name Islamism so that Muslims like me are confronted with a stark choice. Either we reclaim our religion and its narrative or allow thugs and demagogues to speak in its name and impose it on others. Merely calling it "extremism" is too relative and vague, and sidesteps the responsibility to counter its scriptural justification.

It is no surprise, therefore, that any intervention by the international community, no matter how carefully planned, is successfully stigmatized by

Islamists before a grassroots audience of Muslims. The Islamist narrative that the "West" is at war with "Islam" settles better among societies that have been primed with decades of Islamist proselytizing. This is partly why it is so important for regional Muslim-led allies to fight the Islamic State themselves. The success of this Islamist narrative results in a lose/lose scenario for international action. To take Syria as an example, a failure to intervene in its civil war was construed as the "West's" indifference to Muslim suffering, while intervening would have been construed as "Western" imperialism. Either scenario could be used to recruit more jihadists. He who dictates the narrative sets the terms.

The only way, in the long run, to prevent this is by facilitating a genuine grassroots movement to popularize alternative narratives that can compete with Islamist ones. This is why we set up Khudi in Pakistan. But such initiatives must be encouraged across the region. An authentic and indigenous cultural shift is needed, and this will require years of work. Currently, the work to reform Muslim identity, scriptural interpretations, and cultural affiliations, and to discredit the Islamist ideology, is many decades behind.

Harris So the first challenge is to spread a commitment to secularism in Muslim communities, East and West. But many Muslims associate secularism with oppression—Western *and* Muslim. As you know, in many countries the alternative to Islamism has been secular dictatorship. How do you get 1.6 billion Muslims to distinguish the promise of secularism from the tyrannies of Gaddafi, the Shah of Iran, Saddam Hussein, Musharraf, and the rest?

Nawaz What you have raised is a real challenge. If I argue that the solution to Islamism and Muslim fundamentalism lies in encouraging pluralism, which leads to secularism, which leads to liberalism, then how do we de-stigmatize secularism when it has been so abused by Arab *Ba'thist* dictators? The stigma is so bad that there is not even an accurate word for secularism in Urdu. The word used is *la-deeniyat*, which is derived from the Arabic, meaning "no-religionism." I've often suggested introducing *'almaaniyyah* into Urdu, which is a more neutral Arabic equivalent for the word secularism. The situation has deteriorated even more since the Arab Uprisings because democracy led to Islamists gaining a majority in Egypt, and this led to another secular Arab coup taking matters back to square one.

To start with, we could point to Tunisia. This birthplace of Arab Uprisings witnessed an Islamist-inspired government voluntarily cede power and allow for a secular party with the largest vote share to form a government after them. The Islamist-inspired party Hizb al-Nahda had paved the way for such a development because when forming their own government immediately after the uprising, they dropped the clause stipulating that a version of *shari'ah* must form the basis for law. If Hizb al-Nahda's more mature approach to post-Islamist politics can spread to neighboring Egypt, and then the region, much good could come from it.

But all the onus cannot be on the Islamists. Ruling Arab secular strongmen must bear a great deal of the burden. They should work with post-Islamist factions that are akin to Hizb al-Nahda in each country to build on the Tunisian model and to encourage a more democratic approach across the region. To achieve this, a combination of political, intellectual, and cultural approaches are necessary. The international community cannot afford to let the chance for secular democracy in the

Middle East slip into oblivion for another fifty years.

None of this can work, however, if there is no demand for secular democracy at the grassroots level. This is why it is vital that a new social contract is negotiated by Arabs, for Arabs, on the Arab street. Here's where I believe that the Khudi model we initiated in Pakistan, which I referred to earlier, becomes relevant. I tried to lay the intellectual basis for what such an effort could look like in my TED talk, and only hope that others take up this cause and make it their own.

Harris And how do you see us increasing the demand for secular democracy at the grassroots level if both secularism and democracy are so often viewed as an assault upon religious identity?

Nawaz This is only possible with a combination of cultivating more Muslim reform voices—along with more liberal, ex-Muslim, and non-Muslim voices that are willing to speak critically about these issues. Each of these is sorely lacking, while the far-right critique is rising. Therefore, the liberal and "moderate" Muslim concern to "support" Muslims against extremism, by pandering and equivocating, is only harming Muslims and aiding extremists, as proponents on the far right are the only ones consistently seen to be challenging anything.

Harris That last point has been one of my greatest concerns for over a decade. As daunting as the project of reforming Islam is, it cannot even begin if the way forward is thought to be a choice between wishful thinking on one hand and bigotry on the other. I'm very grateful that you've taken the time to explore a third path with me, Maajid—where the conversation between a Muslim and a non-Muslim can begin with a frank admission of the full scope and actual dynamics of the problem of Muslim intolerance. Beliefs matter. It's amazing that the point needs to even be made—but it does, again and again. And the only hope of moving beyond the current religious chaos, through pluralism and secularism, and finally to a convergence on liberal values, is to modify the beliefs of millions of people through honest conversation.

It's a conversation that I've very much enjoyed having with you, Maajid, and I hope it's only the first of many. Needless to say, I wish you the best of luck with all your endeavors.

Nawaz Allow me to take this opportunity to also thank you, Sam. It isn't easy for anyone to reach across divides—real or imagined—and to try and hold a sensible dialogue amid so much background noise and confusion. You will no doubt be censured by some Islam critics for not insisting that I am in fact a closet jihadist, just as I will be criticized by many Muslims for having this conversation with you.

I have nevertheless enjoyed being able to air these issues together, and I too hope this dialogue sets the precedent for many such conversations going forward, and that many others take up such a task. This is an alternative to the violence we see all around us, and ultimately can be the only way forward. Reforming our approach to Islam in the modern age is a huge task, but it has to start somewhere.

My colleagues and I are attempting to inspire people to think and speak like this, which is why we've set up Quilliam. I wrote my memoir *Radical* as a rallying cry for others. I want them to read and understand that I came at this with no animosity or bad intentions. I came at this after beginning as an Islamist and trying to achieve what many

Islamists today still strive for. I'm hoping my journey will encourage people to give us that chance, to just listen to and hear what we're saying, and engage with us so that together we can move in a more positive direction. And may you go in peace, Sam.

FURTHER READING

The following list of suggested readings offers further support for the positions we take in our dialogue. We offer it in the hope that our readers will deepen their understanding of these issues and continue the conversation.

—SH & MN

1. The Qur'an
2. *Radical* by Maajid Nawaz
3. *The End of Faith* by Sam Harris
4. *Who Needs an Islamic State?* by Abdelwahab el-Affendi
5. *Why I Am Not a Muslim* by Ibn Warraq
6. *Freedom of Religion, Apostasy & Islam* by Abdullah Saeed and Hassan Saeed
7. *Terror and Liberalism* by Paul Berman
8. *A Guide to Refuting Jihadism: Critiquing Radical Islamist Claims to Theological Authenticity* by Hannah Stuart and Rashad Ali
9. *Infidel* by Ayaan Hirsi Ali
10. *Reason, Freedom, and Democracy in Islam* by AbdolKareem Soroush

ACKNOWLEDGMENTS

The authors wish to thank (in alphabetical order) Ayaan Hirsi Ali, Faisal Saeed Al Mutar, Jerry Coyne, Richard Dawkins, Annaka Harris, Dr. Usama Hasan, Tom Holland, Thomas LeBien, Rachel Maggart, Ali A. Rizvi, and Martha Spaulding for their very helpful notes on the text.

INDEX